HOW TO BE A
BADASS
FEMALE
CEO

SLAY THE COMPETITION
AND REACH THE TOP

MIMI MACLEAN

launch pad
PUBLISHING

DISCLAIMER

This work is non-fiction and, as such, reflects the author's memory of the experiences.

To all the Badass entrepreneurial women out there who are trying to make their dreams a reality

and

To my family

CONTENTS

THE BADASS CEO BOOK BONUS MATERIALS

Scan this code for supplemental videos and resources to compliment *The Badass CEO* book.

INTRODUCTION

We tell little girls—our daughters, nieces, students, even girls we don't know but silently root for—that they can be anything they want to be.

If you have a daughter (or have been a daughter), you've probably said or heard some version of this: *you can be a ballerina, you can be an astronaut, you can be president, you can be a CEO, you can have a family, you can have it all.*

As of 2021, that aspirational statement is coming ever closer to reality. We have a female vice president, more women earn college degrees than their male counterparts, Misty Copeland is the country's first African American prima ballerina and to date 52 women have been launched into space as astronauts.

In one generation, women went from being shut

out of the labor force to comprising more than 50 percent of employed Americans. Many working women are also moms, and while it might be exhausting, tons of working mothers feel like superheroes who show the world that they *can* have it all.

Women-founded companies are killing it, too: studies show that they're earning, on average, two times the revenue per dollar invested compared with companies founded by men. Everywhere you turn, women are making waves and making money in virtually every industry, from tech to finance and from fashion to film. Actresses and models, long expected to look pretty and do little else, are branching out into producing, investing and product development. For the first time in history, so many aspects of women's lives are no longer a hindrance to succeeding in business but are actually helping them get ahead. By every possible metric, there's never been a better time to be a female CEO, or a woman at the start of her career with her eyes fixed firmly on the top job.

If you've read this far and thought, "Okay...when is the other shoe going to drop?"

Get ready.

Remember when I pointed out that more than 50 percent of the workforce is made up of women? Guess how many of them hand out business cards that say "CEO, CFO or CMO"?

5.2 percent.

Fifty percent of the workforce but only five percent of leadership. As for jobs that lead to powerful positions, the statistics aren't much better. According to a recent *Forbes* study, men outnumber women in C-suite positions by a ratio of 17 to 1. And half of the companies that participated in the study had *no* women in C-level roles. At all. At so many major corporations, studies show, women occupy jobs that don't lead to high-level promotions, while men are often set on the leadership track from the day they sign their offer letters.

If you're thinking something like "that's just the corporate world! I'm going to have my *own* business," you aren't out of the woods. Only 1.7 percent of women-led businesses do a million dollars in sales, and only three percent of women-founded companies get venture capital money, according to a 2020 Crunchbase study. The VC world, too, has a woman problem: just 10 percent of partners at major VC firms are women.

As an angel investor, I've spent my entire career—and in many ways, my entire life—contemplating this problem, and I want to help you push beyond it. I want to see women smash sales goals year after year, taking their ingenious inventions and gorgeous designs into markets all around the globe. I want to see women who start out as entry-level assistants end up at the head of the boardroom table, remaking the image of the CEO into one that's fierce, feminine and running things on her own terms.

I know that's a tall order, but I think we can get there. First, we have to figure out what's holding so many talented, smart, capable women back. I know that's not always easy. I know it's not possible to add more hours to the day, keep kids from getting sick the morning of important presentations or make dinner magically appear on the table every night so you can have an extra hour to grind out emails.

But I do see a lot of the same problems when women strike out on their own, and I'm not going to pull any punches calling them out in this book. If you're:

- Not thinking big enough
- Having a hard time nailing down a strategy
- Unsure of how to find and best utilize outside investments
- Not tapping into your network to look for mentors, sounding boards and potential partnerships
- Insisting on wearing too many hats
- Letting imposter syndrome stop you before you've even begun

- Trying to achieve perfection when what you really need is to just do it already
- Putting yourself and your business last

We're going to talk about it! Let's take the issue of mentorship, for example: did you know that 79 percent of high-level businessmen point to a mentor who has helped them grow professionally? Only 45 percent of business*women* say the same thing, which means there are thousands of women at work *right now* not taking advice that could change their careers forever—because they don't even know they should be getting it in the first place.

So how do I know all of this? On my podcast, The Badass CEO, I interview women who are hustling, financing and bootstrapping their own businesses. Many of them started from scratch, and more than one started from her own kitchen. Along the way, they've faced challenges you can imagine and challenges you can't, and with me they're ready to talk about the good, the bad and the ugly. That way, you, the woman who wants to be a CEO and *knows she can do it*, can reap the benefits of their hard-won expertise.

We also get into the *whys* of all of this, and for me, it's personal. I've had almost every kind of job under the sun, working at one of New York's most prestigious investment banking firms and also at one of New

York's most famous department stores. I got an MBA from Columbia Business School, where I was recognized for my deep understanding of and connection to the entrepreneurial mindset. I've started three companies, and I've invested in even more, focusing on women-led businesses that innovate and solve problems that other businesses didn't even know existed. I've also kept an open mind, taking chances on people, products and industries more traditional investors might have written off.

Like so many other women in business, I'm also a mom. I know what it's like to be exhausted at the end of the day and to think, "B*etween homework and soccer practice and college applications, I simply won't have time to focus on my CEO ambitions.*"

If any of this rings a bell, I want to help. Maybe you've always dreamed of having your own business. Or maybe you love to create but are unsure of how to turn your inspiration into something bigger. Maybe you're reading this on your lunch break at a day job you know isn't the One, or maybe you're reading it after the kids are in bed, fantasizing about the day you'll be the boss at home *and* at work.

Or maybe just maybe you don't know what you want, but you're ready to find out. To try, to fall, and to learn how to pick yourself back up again.

To some day have employees who look up to you. "Our CEO?" they'll say.

"She's a badass."

IDENTIFY AND FOSTER YOUR ENTREPRENEURIAL SPIRIT

You might need to hear this: you have permission to make your own rules when it comes to work. You don't love working all the time? That's okay: figure out a life where work isn't the be-all, end-all and focus on getting there.

But if you're like me and *do* love to work—much like many of the women I interview on my podcast—I think it's time you consider what kind of work really thrills you. That's the kind of work you'll really thrive in.

Let me do you one better: it's totally okay to say, "I never want to work in an office" or "I never want to work for someone else." I'm telling you this because I want you to accept who you are and to have confidence in yourself.

There's so much about the world, about work and

about our own lives that we can't control. It's easy to get hung up on those things, especially when it comes to our careers: not making enough money, not having flexible hours and not getting enough time to develop our own ideas.

What you can control, though, is your story, your confidence, your sense of self and what you want.

When you own your story and have confidence in what you want, investors are going to believe in you. If you're still conflicted about your vision, the sort of work-life balance you want and the kind of company you want to build, you're not ready to ask people to invest in you—and that's okay. Entrepreneurship is a full-time job. It's like having a child to nurture. We'll get you there.

Here's something I learned early on when I started working at one of my first jobs: the idea of working at the same place for the same people for decades makes me want to run screaming into the ocean.

My father, on the other hand, was a tax accountant for Arthur Andersen for 40 years. He had a big family to take care of—I'm one of six, so sticking with a fulfilling and great paying job for his entire adult life made sense for him. For me, though? I would wither into a gray blob of discontent. It's not the routine that would kill my spirit or seeing the same coworkers at the same work parties for a quarter century; it's the lack of adventure. What excites me about entrepreneurs and business ventures is the thrill of ideas. I find *ideas*— their development, planning, implementation, failure, reboots and wild successes—to be the greatest adventures in life.

My first year out of college I went to work as an investment banker at Kidder Peabody, where I threw myself into the working world and the fast-paced New York City lifestyle with gusto.

I was 24 years old, flying on private jets around the world with high-powered executives and working 90 hours a week doing investment banking deals, raising capital for some of the biggest companies in the world. I was working on Initial Public Offerings (also known as IPOs, which is when a company goes from being privately held to being on the stock market, where anyone can buy shares and gain a stake) as well as debt and private offerings. Financial modeling is what I did all day long, trying to project the income and valuation of these companies. I charted the course of these massive revenue streams through peaks and valleys. And while I could tell you about the finances of each company inside and out, I couldn't exactly tell you *why they were able to accomplish this success*. It was exhilarating, seeing these companies reach the scale they did. A good idea coupled with hard work and proper leadership made a company big enough to go public, and I was fascinated by the journey. I had *so many* questions. How does a person build something like this? How do you even build something that's a *fraction* as successful? I was looking at the end product of 200 years of exquisitely refined global capitalism. I was hungry for ideas and innovation. I loved seeing the culmination of an entrepreneur's dream into the ultimate exit, and it made me want to be an entrepreneur, to see what I could build on my own. It's also where the seeds of the work I do now were planted—I learned that I wanted to be my own boss, making my own rules and my own way in the world.

Still, I wasn't quite sure how that was going to look in practice. From Kidder Peabody I went to Price Waterhouse, one of New York's biggest accounting firms, where I also obtained my CPA, learning about accounting, auditing and how taxes work when you're a mega-corporation. And two years after *that*, I pivoted once more, going into Bloomingdale's prestigious buyer's program, a kind of bootcamp (albeit a pretty glamorous one) where new recruits were trained to understand every aspect of the mega-department store's operations. I wanted to learn how to *really* run a business. As an assistant buyer for the national department store, I helped with the eye-popping budget and the responsibility of selecting merchandise for over 20 stores. I was also responsible for analyzing market trends, purchasing product assortment, managing sales and margins, contract negotiations, inventory management, sales planning, forecasting and coordinating closely with the merchandising and operations teams. It was fascinating work that taught me how to truly understand the fundamentals of operating a successful business.

It also paid me about a third of what I was making in finance.

"You're doing this all wrong," my dad told me, laughing. "You're supposed to be making more money each year, not less." My dad said I was fickle. He might have been right, but the experience was invaluable. I was surrounded by ideas, details and the well-oiled machine of a globally recognizable brand that was over 100 years old. Every department had a specific job to do, and as a buyer I was able to learn a bit of everything, rapidly filing away knowledge and knowing that someday I'd count this among my most valuable experiences.

While I loved working at Bloomingdale's, I knew I wasn't going to be there forever, which is partly why I decided my path was headed in the direction of business school. I'm nothing if not ambitious, so I buckled down to work on applications and soon found myself a student at Columbia Business School, one of the country's most elite programs and one that regularly churns out future CEOs of companies old and new. While I was there, I focused on entrepreneurship—I knew I didn't want to go back into finance or accounting, or even to a corporate job at a place like Bloomingdale's again. Whatever my future held, it was going to be one of my own making.

Having won the business plan competition at Columbia Business School, I jumped headfirst into the world of being my own boss, starting an internet company and then a few other companies after that (more on those later) and eventually finding my calling as an angel investor.

As I grew older and started a family, the fact that I loved *ideas* came into clear focus. I saw then that I wanted to help nurture, fund and evangelize great ideas. When I'm tied to just one idea, one plan or one product, I'm not happy and not successful. You may be like this, too.

Then again, you may not. And that's the question we're here to ask: *what do you want your work life to look like?*

How to Conceptualize Fantasy Work Life

Let's pinpoint what sort of role you want to play in starting your own business.

There really are no right or wrong answers. Not sure where to start? Sample some of these scenarios:

- You love the idea of being a true mogul. You want to start with one product or idea but quickly diversify until you have an empire, raising the funds on your own in the beginning and then looking for investors to help you get to the next level. In your ultimate fantasy, you're ringing the bell at the New York Stock Exchange on the day your company goes public.
- You have an idea you'd like to see through to the final stages—a product, an invention, a service no one but you can offer. You want to get it off the ground and run your own company, bootstrapping all aspects of the business because it's important to you to have something that's *yours*.
- You have a mind for business, whether it's been honed in traditional office jobs or on another path. You don't necessarily have *the* idea right now, but you know your future is one in which you're the boss.

Wherever you are on your journey, asking these questions can go a long way toward clarifying what exactly it is you want out of work—and what you have to give.

Still not sure? Ask yourself these questions. You can skip to the back of the book to see some more sample questions/answers to get your creative embers sparking. Don't hold back, go big :

- What do I want my workdays to look like?
- What sort of relationship do I want to have with my company?
- What are the responsibilities I want to take on?
- What are the responsibilities I absolutely *do not* want to take on?
- What sort of experience do I want consumers to have with my company/product/service?
- Who are the types of people that will work for my company?
- What qualities will my best employees have?
- What qualities will my employees absolutely *not* have?
- What sort of relationship do I want to have with my employees?
- What does my time off from my job look like?

- How do I want to feel about my work at the end of a week?
- How do I want my family to feel about my work?

Some Badass Advice on Your Work Life

Which brings us to the next big point I want to make: being the boss is hard. It's something that requires, above all else, dedication. My life, for example, comes with a lot of flexibility. I can take my kids to school, go on an impromptu vacation and work from my pajamas at the kitchen counter. While you might look at me and just see a life of leisure, you're not seeing that I'm thinking about my next big meeting on every drive, answering emails on every beach chair and at that kitchen counter *all day long*.

What life looks like when you're the boss is something that comes up on my podcast a lot. "I think probably the thing that I've had to give up and that you continue to give up is my own personal downtime," Rosie Johnston, whose company By Rosie Jane makes clean, sustainable fragrances sold in stores like Sephora. "When you're an entrepreneur, it just doesn't exist. Whether you're on vacation, whether you're at home, whether you're sick, getting married, giving birth, everything stops with you. So I think you give away a little bit of your peace of mind when you become an entrepreneur."

In so many ways, having a company is like having a child—it needs attention, care and sometimes even a little tough love. But above all, being an entrepreneur means that the business needs you.

That can mean spending some time teaching yourself how to work smarter, like Stacy Verbeist, founder and CEO of W!nk, the first therapeutic cannabis line created by women, for women. "I was a concentrated worker," Verbeist told me when I interviewed her. "I could get more done in three hours than someone could in eight hours! You know, if the kids are going to be in school from eight to three, I've got to fit in my workout. I've got to fit in my phone calls. I've got to fit in my paperwork and mailers and everything else that I have to do. And then be there and be able to let go when they come home, and open the door when they get in and be so happy. And then get them through dinner and to bed. And then maybe start working again for a few hours. You just have to do what works for you."

Just like a happy baby has happy parents, being a CEO is a lesson in remembering something I see so many people—especially women—try to ignore: you have to put yourself first if this is going to work in the long term.

Verbeist, whose business deals with self-care, seconds this. "The biggest thing to being an entrepreneur is being able to alleviate stress and self-care," she told me. "If you do not take care of yourself, your family and your business are not going to get anywhere. Even if it's just 15 minutes a day. Even if it's going on a walk, whatever you do, you've got to put yourself first."

I say all of this not to scare you: although if you're at the beginning of your career or your career pivot, I know it can sound pretty scary. I say it because knowing who you are, what you want and what you're capable of is half the battle in reaching your goals. Knowing your limits is equally important: if the idea of doing this all on your own, and of having the future of an entire company resting on your shoulders, is some-thing that makes you want to run away screaming, you don't have to force it.

There's no reward without some risk, and for so many of us with entrepreneurial minds, the rewards are immeasurable, both at work and at home. Because being the boss might mean working all the time, but it also might mean prioritizing your own values. For Celeste Markey, cofounder and CEO of Careste, a San Francisco–based direct-to-consumer fashion startup that creates chic, sustainable clothing on-demand, those values include the sanctity of family dinner.

"We try to have family dinner together every night without fail," Celeste shared on my podcast. "And our rule at family dinner is that there are no devices allowed to dinner. That it's like our 30 minutes to an hour of just plain togetherness, no interruptions. And what I love about our dinner table is that we go around and we talk about what our favorite part of the day was. And my kids are six and three, so it gets a little entertaining, especially with the three-year-old."

That's something being your own boss can offer—the ability to work and live on your own terms.

2

DON'T QUIT YOUR DAY JOB—YET

Here's a question I get asked all the time: *should I start a business while working or not?* Unless you create a truly ingenious product or service (e.g., Facebook) from scratch, you need to learn the market you're trying to disrupt, dominate or simply break into. It's also an opportunity to see how other people handle challenges and to use those challenges to stretch your own ideas risk-free.

So my short answer is, don't quit your day job—yet.

Now here's my longer, more useful, answer.

I knew fairly early on in my career (and in my life itself) that I wanted to strike out on my own. Frustratingly, the world of business was pretty different 30 years ago, and there weren't a ton of options for someone who wanted to blaze her own trail, be the boss and raise a family. So I did what millions of other people did after college: I packed up, moved out and got a job. As you know by now, I tried on a number of roles, but looking back, I think I was too quick to jump ship once I realized something wasn't the right fit.

That's not to say I should have stayed forever in a job I didn't love, and that's not the advice I'm giving you now. What I mean is that if I could tell my sleep-deprived, workaholic 26-year-old self something about what her future would look like, it would be to get ready to make some real mistakes. If I could give her a piece of advice, it would be to make some of those mistakes on someone else's dime.

I would say to her, or to any other aspiring entrepreneur, "*Stick with it. Not forever, but until you've learned all you can to make your next move a success.*" At the time, I was too itchy and afraid of getting trapped in an uninspiring career or one that didn't match the lifestyle I wanted, so I bolted before I could wring out every bit of knowledge from my surroundings. I mean, I was working at some pretty big-deal places—places that were full of case studies and colleagues who could have taught me so much about business, marketing, sales, systems and what my life might look like with me at the helm of my own company. I was also in my 20s, which is when you *should* be working your tail off. So, if you are in your 20s and reading this, put your energy into your career now. Don't worry about your social life so much. Because the time you spend on your career early on will put you leaps and bounds ahead of others your age who are out clubbing and partying.

Now, as an angel investor, when I meet an entrepreneur who is looking to carve out their own niche in a market, I want to make sure they really understand that market. The more mastery they have, the more I'm likely to invest. I want to see that people are experienced, connected and have done some serious learning. And if part of learning is making mistakes, why make them on your dollar when you can make them on someone else's? Or better yet, watch people who have more responsibility—and make more money than you—make their own mistakes. This way you can get a firsthand look at what it's like to be at the top.

Stefanie Cove is the founder of Stefanie Cove and Company, a global event design and production company. Cove has masterminded events for Net-a-Porter and Diane von Furstenberg, and she has been crowned "the very best planner around" by Goop. When she was a guest on my podcast, one of the things she wanted to convey to listeners is that experience is something that you can never have enough of. "In the hospitality industry, I personally feel like the experience is much more important than school. I think school is great obviously, and I enjoyed my college experience, but I think that this kind of learning you get only through life," she said. "And I think if you don't know what part of the business you want to work in, work for a hotel that has all the different components, such as food and beverage, rooms division, events, et cetera. If you really love food and beverage, move over to a restaurant, learn more from the chefs. If you like the events, I would work for an event producer as an intern for a while to understand that aspect before you can get an entry level position in that field and start to build your way up."

What's another example of learning on the job? Let's say it's your dream to open a boutique fitness studio. You've got the moves down, the playlists ready and a perfect location. Maybe if you're really lucky, you've even got some money to invest. The fact that you've never actually run a business before is totally irrelevant—you know in your bones that your classes are going to be hugely in demand. And everything else? It'll work itself out.

Then, before you know it, it's Day One of the rest of your life. Beyoncé is cued up on the state-of-the-art sound system you had installed and you're ready to welcome your first group of workout-obsessed women into your space. But:

- Your computer system is glitching, making it hard for people to sign up in advance.
- The location you picked out is on a fantastic block, but your classes are 90 minutes, and the whole street is lined with One Hour Parking signs.
- The class times you chose conflict with school drop-off, making it hard for local moms to get to you on time.
- Gosh—isn't it hot in here? Is the air conditioning working? Did you remember to stock the fridge with bottled water and to set up a petty cash drawer so that when someone wants to pay for one of those bottled waters with a $20 bill, you can give them change?
- Oh, and the instructor you hired based on her bubbly personality? The one whose references you forgot to contact. Wasn't she supposed to be here half an hour ago?

I'm not saying all of this is going to happen on the day of your grand opening—but it very well could.

How would you (the version of you who is green to the business world) handle this stuff being thrown at you? What happens when one of your customers gets a parking ticket and takes it out on you via a particularly unkind Yelp review? What resources do you have to draw on to move forward?

Now let's turn back the clock to when your business was a fresh, new idea you were working on. What if you decided to get a job teaching classes at one of your city's hottest spin studios, where you'd have to wear a uniform and work according to someone else's schedule but also have the chance to experience every aspect of the business? Maybe you'd learn things like:

- How to troubleshoot the most common software used in the fitness industry
- What time of day classes were most crowded and which time slots were usually empty
- How the studio you work for handles things like parking and storage and how they set up a waiting area for customers to hang out in
- Who to call when there's a problem with the space and how to solve some of those problems before they arise
- How to spot signs of a flaky coworker, so that when you're the one doing the hiring and firing, you know exactly what questions to ask

Which version of your future business do you think is going to be more successful? The one where you learn while doing, or the one where you've learned before you do, bringing with you a breadth of knowledge you *literally got paid to learn?*

Working for someone else is a great opportunity to play detective, both about your industry and your very own business plan.

Here are four things you can do while you develop your business plan and become an expert in your field.

Identify the Right Conditions for a Pivot

Does Nobu sell sushi, or do they sell a luxury experience?

Is Crossfit a gym or a community that thrives on accountability?

Does a day spa sell facials, or does it offer a place where women can relax and feel at peace with their bodies?

Does Tesla sell cars, or do they sell a solution to a larger environmental crisis?

Look at what happened during the COVID-19 pandemic. Studios like Warner Bros. found themselves in an utter crisis. A slate of high-budget films was set to come out in 2020, and then movie theaters across the world shut down for over a year. But what does

Warner Bros. really sell? Popcorn and cramped movie seats? No—they sell stories. The movie studio also took into account the Leichtman Research Group's findings that 78 percent of US homes would have a streaming subscription service and that 55 percent of US homes would have multiple streaming services. On top of that, the typical size for a television in most American homes is 54 inches. So if you're a movie studio that sells big, beautiful stories to be watched in a darkened room, you don't need movie theaters. In December of 2020, Warner Bros. announced that their entire slate of 2021 movies would have theatrical releases (if theaters were open) and would also be streamed exclusively on HBO Max. That means that movies like *Dune, Matrix 4* and *Godzilla vs. Kong* could be all watched at home. It's a pivot that came from a deep understanding of customers, products and the market. When the people who work for Warner Bros. become moguls in their own right, it's a pivot that they'll be able to learn from as they face their own obstacles.

There's no greater pivot story of the 20th century than, of course, Facebook. What started off as a social network for Ivy League college students to share pictures, blog posts and make new friends has turned into one of the most sophisticated data mining and marketing platforms on the planet. Being able to pivot and redefine its goals and strategy has allowed Facebook to become one of the most influential companies in the world.

The key takeaway: Be diligent and constantly evaluate what value your company currently offers while looking toward the future. Long-term success is earned; it's never an accident.

Find Inefficiencies in Your Market and Think of Ways to Solve Them

When I was a buyer at Bloomingdale's in 1999, UPC codes (universal product codes) and stickers were just beginning to be required by all vendors. These vendors would be fined huge amounts of money if their products didn't arrive with the stickers on them. (We required companies, regardless of size, to provide their own stickers.) This was a nightmare for the small startup. Everything was, for the most part, just starting to transition to computers and a universal tracking system. There was no system or company to help vendors, so you can imagine the mix-ups that were a regular part of our jobs—if a rack of black dresses arrived with no stickers, it would take an entire afternoon to sort out. And if a customer called the shoe department, urgently needing to know if we had the exact pair of Stuart Weitzman heels she wanted to wear that same night? Finding such items would not have been as easy as typing the info into a computer like we would today.

The process was totally inefficient and in desperate need of modernization. I remember thinking, "This is madness—we need a better system!" But when I suggested it, people looked at me like I was crazy. I remember calling my dad and telling him I wanted to leave Bloomingdale's to start a company that would create product codes, a database and the technology that the world was heading toward—an innovation that would make the life of vendors *and* buyers easier. He thought it was crazy. I told my husband, and he nodded politely.

Before long, I left Bloomingdale's to start business school. Now, looking back, I think, *Wow, what a missed opportunity.* Imagine if I had stayed, piloted a test program on the side while still working at Bloomingdale's, gone through several iterations until I had a good enough product to leave my job and become a part of the technology SAAS business that is thriving today.

That's what I mean when I say a day job is a great chance to play detective. Look for problems, diagnose inefficiencies and come up with theories on possible solutions. You don't need to have the perfect solution, but having a clear understanding of the problem is a powerful start.

Bring the Five Whys to Every Obstacle You Encounter

Consider the Five Whys method pioneered by Sakichi Toyoda. It was used within the Toyota Motor Corporation during the evolution of its manufacturing methodologies, which are now considered some of the world's most innovative: the Toyota Factory Tour and Museum hosts thousands of visitors each year who travel to Japan just to learn about the company's processes. (Toyotas also regularly dominate the list of America's most popular cars.)

On the surface, it couldn't be simpler: all you have to do is ask why something's not working and then ask why four more times. By the fifth why, you'll have gotten to the root of the problem. So if you currently have a job, start using the Five Whys *today*. Whenever you encounter an obstacle, a failure or a problem, get in the habit of asking why five times to peel back all the layers and get to the root of the issue. Even if it's done just as an exercise for yourself, it'll get you in the habit of problem-solving on a deeper level, which is something you'll need to do when you have your own company.

Let's go back to our future spin studio company. Before diving headfirst into launching your own spin company, you took my advice and opted to work as an instructor for six months to learn everything you can about the boutique spin studio market. When you're not working to develop your business plan, you're an hourly employee teaching eight classes a week on top of a sweaty stationary bike.

Now imagine that there's been big rider demand for a 6 am class at your studio. Your boss finally puts a 6 am class on the schedule, but because there are only 30 bikes, all riders have to preregister for classes, and there's often a waitlist. An email blast goes out to the rider list that the registration for the new 6 am class opens today at noon. Noon comes, the first 10 seats fill up and the site crashes. It takes a full 24 hours to get the site back up. The first 10 riders' seats weren't saved, the class has filled up and now there's a scramble to figure out how to get those 10 initial riders a seat. What a mess.

So start with the Five Whys, and write it out.

Problem Statement: We launched a new class, and it crashed the site.

1. **Why** did the launch crash the site?
   Answer: The server couldn't handle the spike in traffic.
2. **Why** couldn't the server handle the traffic?
   Answer: When the initial website was set

up, the gym owner had the web designer pick the subscription-cloud plan service that was never renewed after the designer completed the initial design. So any spike in traffic could crash the server.

3. **Why** wasn't the subscription renewed after the designer finished their project? Answer: Because the studio owner didn't know it needed to be renewed.

4. **Why** didn't the studio owner know it needed to be renewed? Answer: He was focused on other aspects of his business, but he remembers the designer mentioning something about a cloud service in an email.

5. **Why** didn't the studio owner follow up about the email? Answer: he did not think it was relevant.

You're not looking for blame. It's not a personal issue; it's finding what part of the process went wrong and figuring out how to fix it. The most common way people misuse the Five Whys is by stopping at something simple like "the person in charge was unaware of the issue," which does nothing to evolve their processes and stop the problem from happening again. The key to (and true power of) the Five Whys is creating more efficient systems and processes by learning from your mistakes then figuring out and remedying the actual root of the issue. By sussing out and fixing the cause of a given issue, you're inevitably going to build a more resilient and better system, which is a necessity for creating a thriving business.

Does talking about servers sound as engaging as being on hold with a customer service line? Absolutely, but it's this sort of diligence that pays off. "Success is a function of persistence and doggedness," Malcolm Gladwell says in his book *Outliers*, "and the willingness to work hard for 22 minutes to make sense of something that most people would give up on after 30 seconds."

There will always be unforeseen problems that arise and if there aren't, you're not doing your job as an innovator. But truly successful businesses learn from those problems to build a better system. When you see a problem, look at it as an opportunity to foster your own ingenuity. "Ingenuity is often misunderstood," Atul Gawande writes in his book *Better*. "It is not a matter of superior intelligence but of character. It demands more than anything a willingness to recognize failure, to not paper over the cracks, and to change. It arises from deliberate, even obsessive, reflection on failure."

Utilizing the Five Whys to solve problems, making

sure they don't happen again and creating more efficient processes is the best thing you can do as a business owner. Your problem-solving ability is your power.

Build a Network in the Market You're Breaking Into

I know more than anyone how powerful the need
to be your own boss can be, and I also know the excite-
ment of having a game-changing idea that will catapult
you to the top. But I also know that there are lessons to
be learned everywhere and from everyone and that it's
worth buckling down and taking those lessons in
before you hit the ground running.

Something that comes up a lot on my podcast is the
idea of the network: the group of people in your orbit,
at all levels, who can speak to the quality of your work,
the strength of your ideas and the conviction with
which you see those ideas through.

Recently I chatted with Coral Chung, whose
handbag line Senreve has quickly become a must-have
item for the stylish, on-the-go woman more interested
in quality (Chung's bags, which come in real leather
and vegan leather, are designed in New York and made
in Italy) than flashy labels. Of her early successes,
Chung told me, "I think it was really critical that I
wasn't starting from just a total blank slate. I did have a

lot of advantages going into it. Probably one of the biggest things that was beneficial was actually the relevant network that I had. I was able to get a lot of warm introductions to relevant people, whether it's manufacturing and production or product development or design. And I would say they weren't necessarily just cold outreach or cold LinkedIn outreaches. They were a lot of warm introductions. I was very fortunate to have a lot of advisors, different mentors, and folks in my network who could really just help make these introductions and get these conversations going, which I would say accelerated the process of building Senreve."

Before she launched Senreve in 2015, Chung did stints at Bain & Company and at Prada, building a stellar reputation as a smart, dependable thinker in the worlds of business and fashion along the way. Over the course of her career, she made connections around the world, impressing people with her drive and her know-how. When she was ready to launch Senreve, many of those same people were only too happy to help in any way they could.

That kind of network isn't built overnight, but it's something worth investing in. And if you already have a job, or you're in the process of starting your career, it's one you can get by being willing to listen, ready to learn and, above all, consistent and reliable.

Nellie Aklop, founder of CorpNet, a website that helps small business owners with things like incorporating and corporate compliance, agrees. "Really it all boils down, in my opinion, to consistency. That's the bottom line. You cannot, in my opinion, in this day and age, pay to play. You have to be involved, you have to network yourself. You have to position yourself as an expert in what you're truly an expert at in that field."

As an investor, I couldn't agree more. If I'm going to put my money, my energy and my name behind something, I want to know that the CEO I'm taking a chance on has done their homework, preferably through trial and error. I want to know that they aren't going to quit at the first sign of trouble. I want to know that they've learned the ins and outs of their industry so that they can tell *me* why they're going to change the game.

I have seen some fantastic ideas fail because they were too expensive to produce, raising the retail price above what customers were willing to pay. Or the barrier to entry was too hard in that industry, making it impossible to be successful. These are the kinds of things you need to figure out first, and working for someone else is the perfect time to do that research. As Stefanie Cove puts it: "Build an expertise before you jump in, because it's difficult to jump into a business and run it successfully when you haven't experienced it."

If you're one of the people I talked about earlier— reading this book on your lunch break while you daydream about the day you're running the show—I know it can feel frustrating to imagine waiting even longer to launch the next chapter of your working life. But remember, you don't have to be where you are right now forever: if you're the kind of person who wants it badly enough to pick up this book, there's a good chance you *won't* be where you are right now forever. But while you are here, make the most of it— consider it a gift. Go to every meeting, listen in on every presentation, have lunch with your boss as often as you can. Someday, you *will* be the boss, and you'll look back at the younger version of yourself and be grateful she stuck with it. Then you'll be able to climb the ladder using the muscles you developed along the way.

3

BUILDING YOUR SUPPORT SYSTEM— THE MASTER, THE MENTOR, THE PEERS

If you're an entrepreneur, you might also be a lone wolf. You get frustrated when people can't keep up with your pace. You'd rather spend hours working, scheming about your next idea and being surrounded by other people who have as much zeal for world conquest as you do.

You might be a lone wolf, but someone has to teach baby wolves how to hunt and eat. As an angel investor I want to know: who taught you?

The Master

Unless you've already proven that you can launch successful start-ups, as an investor I want to know that you have someone in your network who you have humbled yourself enough to learn from. I love enthusiasm and the soaring ambition of raw talent, but I also know that solo visionaries who try to do everything on their own often fail and flame out. I've also met entrepreneurs who are so ambitious and in love with their own way of doing things that they only cultivate relationships with people who agree with them and don't challenge them.

So now hear this loud and clear:

You need to find a master.

No, I don't mean a mentor, though you need one of those, too (don't worry—we'll talk about it in a minute). A mentor is an experienced and trusted advisor.

No, I don't mean a guru. A guru is great for unlocking inspiration and pushing through limiting beliefs.

You can and should form meaningful and productive relationships with all of these types of people, but it's critical to seek out a master. A master is someone who has put in their 10,000 hours of work on a particular craft. A master is someone who has spent so much time living, touching, tasting and breathing their craft that their decisions are instinctual. A master has, ahem, *mastery*.

To have mastery means to have *comprehensive knowledge* or skill. How does one achieve comprehensive knowledge? To put it crudely, by screwing up a lot. One of the key requisites of being a master is repeated failures. In his book, *Mastery*, Robert Greene puts it like this:

"There are two kinds of failure. The first comes from never trying out your ideas because you are afraid, or because you are waiting for the perfect time. This kind of failure you can never learn from...The second kind comes from a bold and venturesome spirit. If you fail in this way, the hit that you take to your reputation is greatly outweighed by what you learn. Repeated failure will toughen [the] spirit and show you with absolute clarity how things must be done."

When I talk to an entrepreneur about their business, I want them to tell me what they've *learned* and not what they *know*. I want to know one big mistake they've made that they know how to avoid making again. I'm less interested in how brilliant they are and more interested in how adaptable they are. Can they learn? Can they pivot? Can they be humble enough to see failure as an opportunity and not an insult?

Is a master born with the seeds of dazzling talent that just need a little water, luck and timing to explode? If that were the case, then most people lose the genetic lottery. Instead, I believe, as Greene does, that mastery comes less from raw talent and more from an ability to overcome feeling bored, insecure, frightened or complacent when pursuing your passion.

Ideally, you have the ability to work in the market

where you eventually want to start a business. From there, you want to get yourself onto projects and into roles where you have the greatest possibilities for learning.

You can think of yourself as a student, protégé or novice, but when it comes to your master, I encourage you to think of yourself as an apprentice (no matter how much you're making). Unlike a student, you're not trying to show off for your teacher. Unlike a novice, you're not just a beginner. If you think of yourself as an apprentice—a total blank slate—then you can put your ego aside and enter a phase of deep observation.

As Greene puts it, you need to be willing to revert to a Zen feeling of inferiority: "Zen mind, beginner's mind, if we feel like we already know something or have mastered it, then we stop learning." We need to assume we're beginners and that there's more to learn.

Suze Schwartz, the founder and CEO of Unplug Meditation, the world's first drop-in secular meditation studio, as well as the author of *Unplug: A Simple Guide to Meditation for Busy Skeptics and Modern Soul Seekers*, spoke to me about this mindset during our podcast interview.

"I didn't know anything about anything," she said. "I learned everything as I went along."

"I knew about meditation, but not a lot! I had to find the top teachers in the world to teach [me] and convince them that this was a good idea, because it had never been done before. I had to learn how to work a POS [point of sale] system. I had no idea what that was. I had to buy retail. I never did that before. The fact that everything was a first made it so much fun. Trying all these different things means you have to become an expert."

My favorite part of Schwartz's journey is that she describes the whole thing as "so much fun." She reached out to other people who knew more than she did and came with an apprentice mindset. A key part of your learning journey will always involve learning about the things you don't already know. In Suze's case, her interest in and experience with meditation made it a no-brainer for her to seek out mentors within the field. But what about the rest of it—designing an app, deciding how much to charge for services, building a brand? That's why it's important to look for masters who can speak to your business as a whole and why you never know where you'll find your next master.

I know that true masters are hard to come by, which is why I'm not expecting you to have a ton of potential candidates in your phone's contact list right now. Don't let that discourage you: one thing I love about choosing a master is that sometimes it ends up being someone you've never met (or will never meet). For many women entrepreneurs, someone like Oprah

Winfrey comes to mind—a master of her craft, a master of doing it all and a master of staying focused on herself and her ambitions. Or even Elon Musk: over the course of his career, he solved problems that didn't even exist yet. By choosing a public figure, or a star in your particular industry, you're giving yourself the gift of *imagining yourself as one of them*, which can be a really powerful way to visualize the moment in which you're the master to someone else.

The Mentor

A *great* mentor will never give you the answers to your problems. They will not offer solutions to the obstacles you face. If you call a mentor with a question and they dive into a 10-minute answer, I encourage you to look elsewhere for mentorship. A good mentor gives you prescriptions. A *great* mentor draws those answers out of you. A *great* mentor identifies your strengths and weaknesses. They will develop your ability to put those strengths into play (or those weaknesses to the side), and they will challenge you to think critically about the work you're doing. The best kind of mentor should ask you relentless questions—not to break you down but to push you forward.

A great mentor is like a sports coach. When a baseball player is having trouble hitting the ball during batting practice, does a coach jump into the batting cage, grab the bat from the player and start taking swings for him? Of course not. What would a coach do instead?

They'd make the player an active participant in their own development and success.

I encourage you to look for the type of mentor who won't spoon feed you easy answers. Here's the ideal exchange between mentor and mentee:

Mentee: "How do I solve this?"

Mentor: "How do you think you should solve this?"

Does that sound maddening? Do you just want the answer? I know when I do the *New York Times* crossword, if I see a clue that's too hard or requires me to think for more than 10 seconds, I skip around until I spot an easier one. I wish I could tell you this is some master strategy to solving the puzzle in under 20 minutes. But it's really my unwillingness to do the hard stuff first.

That's the thing about the hard stuff, *it's hard*. As Ben Horowitz writes in his book *The Hard Thing About Hard Things: Building a Business When There Are No Easy Answers*:

"The hard thing isn't setting a big, hairy, audacious goal. The hard thing is laying people off when you miss the big goal...The hard thing isn't setting up an organizational chart. The hard thing is getting people to communicate within the organization that you just designed. The hard thing isn't dreaming big. The hard thing is waking up in the middle of the night in a cold sweat when the dream turns into a nightmare."

Don't undercut your own growth and development by choosing a mentor who does the hard stuff for you.

Like masters, you can find potential mentors in a wide variety of places. Looking for a mentor is a great chance to practice tapping into your own network and really pushing yourself to expand it. Examine your family networks, friendship groups and alumni organizations to look for people who aren't just good at what they do but would be willing to invest in your development.

When you're the head of a successful company, that's when you'll need mentorship the most because you'll constantly be learning new things and handling new challenges. For my podcast I interviewed CEO Brooke Harris, founder of an amazing plant-based milk company called Goodmylk. Harris talked about the role some of her own investors have played in her life. "I'm lucky that most of our investor group is very collaborative and thoughtful and it's a lot of female investors," she said. "So when I have questions or need to talk through that type of stuff, I'll go to them. So our investors are actually the ones who have educated me a lot about the process along the way, and it is like learning a new language."

Above all, a mentor should be someone who brings out the best in you—a person who knows how to help you shine brighter, reach higher and achieve more than you thought you were capable of.

The Peers

Think about over the course of your life, up until now, how many times you've asked a mom, a sister, a roommate or a close friend for advice:

"Does this skirt go with this top?"

"Should I say yes to a second date?"

"Which school district should we move into?"

Whether it's a big decision, a small decision or a decision that feels both big *and* small, we rely on our networks to help us work through the pros and cons, knowing that at the end of the day the people we're turning to are people who want what's best for us—and are people who are asking us for advice in return.

If you're not developing a similar network in your professional life, you're seriously missing out.

Whether you're an investment banker or a lawyer, a baker or a programmer, a stay-at-home mom or are married to your job, a group of peers—people who are at the same stage of the game as you, or fairly close to it

—is an invaluable resource, one you can tap into for contractor recommendations, investor feedback or even gut-checks on whether or not a potential deal or move feels right.

It's also one where you'll develop leads for your business and be able to offer others leads in return. Let's say you're working on a skincare line, and someone in your peer group just opened her own holistic health-care center. For you, her business might be the perfect place to stock your serums and potions, and for her, your products might be a great way to branch out into the world of retail.

The great thing about peers is that you can find them everywhere: think about people you went to college with, the cohort from your first internship, the parents of your kid's friends. Let your friends and family play matchmaker: does your mother play tennis with someone whose own daughter just finished business school? Do your boyfriend's friends have girlfriends interested in joining a business-focused book club?

In fact, here's an exercise you can do right now (or right after you've finished reading this chapter, if you'd rather wait).

Log into your LinkedIn account—and if you don't have one, set it up ASAP. I'll wait!

Do a few keyword searches based on your professional interests and your own background—think about where you went to college, a company you once worked for or even your hometown. Come up with a list of five people who fall into different categories. A few suggestions to get you started:

- A college classmate who had the same major as you
- Someone who went to your high school and is now living in the city or town where you live
- A former coworker now running her own business
- A friend of a friend whose work is complementary to yours—an editor if you're a writer, a product manager if you're a product designer, a salesperson if you're in marketing
- A person who does what you currently do for a company you'd love to work with someday
- A distant relative you've never actually talked business with
- A mom you met at a kid-focused event who is taking time out of the workforce but has a seriously impressive background

Send each of them a message asking if they'd like to chat about work sometime! Share an article they might find interesting, offer to tell them something about your work, ask them a question about news in their industry —whatever feels most natural to you. Reaching out can be scary, but if you get even *one* response, that's one peer you now have a budding relationship with.

Building your peer support network is also something you can do in your existing friend groups. If you have a standing lunch or happy hour with a friend or group of friends, why not suggest you make the next one career-centric, where everyone gets the chance to talk about their professional lives and ask for help strategizing about things like how to ask for a raise or how to solicit early-stage feedback on a new product.

Or why not try becoming active in the kind of group designed exactly for this kind of networking?

- The local chapter of your college's alumni group, or an alumni chapter of your sorority or school sports team
- A volunteer group like the Junior League
- A Toastmasters group, where the focus is on building and developing public speaking skills
- A Mastermind group: based on a philosophy developed in the 1920s, which

uses peer-to-peer mentoring to help members individually and collectively achieve goals

- Most coworking spaces host social events where members can meet and chat about their start-ups. More coworking spaces exclusively for women are popping up in major cities, and most of them emphasize networking. If you currently work from home, why not join one? Not only would it be a good excuse to get out of the house, but you'd have a chance to meet like-minded, business-focused people.

One of the things I love about doing my Badass CEO podcast is that it functions as a sort of virtual peer group for both guests and listeners. Many of my guests are women who bootstrapped their own companies and turned their ideas into successful brands. But they're also women who are focused on what's next. We talk about their successes and how they got to where they are today, but we also talk about the challenges they've faced and the challenges they're currently facing: whether or not to scale, how fast to expand and, recently, how their businesses have been impacted by rapid changes in the global economy. And that's what I want for your peer group: problem-solvers just as ready to ask for advice as to offer it and those with whom you can be open, vulnerable and excited, knowing that each member of the group is focused on mastering their craft and dominating their chosen industry.

4

PROGRESS, NOT PERFECTION

Most women tend to be perfectionists. I am not saying *all* women, but I think we tend to focus on details more than men. I also think this is one reason we as women aren't reaching the higher positions and successes we talked about earlier. Instead of moving forward, launching and growing, we dwell on small details that don't really matter. We want everything to be absolutely perfect before we introduce it into the world. However, this mentality is wrong. This is your view of what perfect is, not the customer's.

Have you heard the saying "Good enough never is"? It's an inspirational management cliché, a rallying call for employees to do better. It helps team members develop the courage to stand up for quality when they're on a collision course with a high-stakes deadline.

But what if sometimes this "good enough" adage is actually true? In his book *The Lean Start Up*, Eric Ries tells the story of Google Maps. The development team was showing the senior management at Google a rudimentary version of a new map program. According to Silicon Valley lore, CEOs Larry Page and Sergey Brin simply said, "It's already good enough. Ship it." Ries writes, "The team complied despite their reservations and fear. And the rest is history: Google Maps was a huge success. This success was aided by the fact that it did just one thing extremely well—its lack of extra features emphasized its differentiation. Shipping sooner accentuated this difference, and it took competitors a long time to catch up."

To succeed, Ries argues a point that I wholeheartedly endorse: entrepreneurs need to be willing to find a spot on the spectrum between "ship anything soonest" to "always build it right, no matter what it takes."

The Consumer Defines Quality

What we define as "quality" has evolved dramatically in the digital age. So many of our ideas about quality are rooted in 19th-century manufacturing. When people think of quality products, they think of reliable items made from solid parts that don't break down, wear out or fail out of nowhere. In today's world,

Ries writes, "Quality is often defined by factors beyond reliability: design, ease of use, aesthetic appeal and convenience." In other words, the customer is the most important part of the production line. This means that quality is in the eye of the customer—not created by the producers who know each and every one of a product's tiny flaws.

It's not just something we say in business, either. *Saturday Night Live* has been on television for 46 seasons, and in that time, many of its biggest stars have published memoirs detailing their careers and their experiences on the iconic comedy show. There's one saying attributed to producer Lorne Michaels that almost everyone recalls as having a huge impact on the way they thought about work:

"The show doesn't go on because it's ready. The show goes on because it's 11:30 on Saturday night."

Creatives can easily get stuck wanting to make whatever they're working on the best it can be. But, as an *SNL* creative, have you really succeeded if you're still tinkering at 11:35 on a Saturday night?

Try your best to take your mind out of the perfectionist head space and think of yourself as the consumer you already are. Let's say there's a cooking app that you use and like. It gives you recipes and allows you to bookmark them. It doesn't allow you to organize the bookmarks—they all appear in one long list ordered alphabetically (as opposed to being divided by type of meal or cuisine), but you still use it several nights a week. When there's an upgrade three months down the line that adds the ability to sort your recipe list by breakfast, lunch and dinner, you download it and are pleased. You didn't delete the app, and maybe you even wrote a review that helped the designers think of better improvements. You still like your imperfect app.

Designers of the app may *only* see the fact that an algorithm to differentiate between Mediterranean and Middle Eastern dishes isn't working or that the sans-serif font shows up wonky on Android phones. They get stuck toiling under the misguided notion that quality means perfection. Very few startups fail for lack of technological sophistication. They almost always fail for lack of customers. If you don't have customers, then you will have a warped sense of what quality is. Instead of asking what the perfect version of your product can be, ask yourself, *What will the customer care about? How will they define quality?*

Ries argues that instead of perfection, entrepreneurs should focus instead on the "minimum viable product." This is the version of the product that will allow a team to collect the maximum amount of customer feedback with the least effort.

As an investor, I know how hard and expensive it is

to get customers. I'm less interested in your quest for perfection and more concerned with your plan to be iterative—how you'll learn from your customers and adapt to *their* notions of quality. As Haas School of Business professor Stephen Blank puts it in his Customer Development Manifesto, "In a startup, no facts exist inside the building, only opinions." You don't have to give up on the quest for the perfect product, but you do need to get out of the building and put your product in the field. What you think the customer wants might not be what the customer really wants, so you wasted time and resources trying to perfect what *you* thought they wanted. Just launch your product and adapt to what they want.

Tamra Johnson is the CEO and cofounder of Flex-Team, a global network of women in business who work in teams, consulting for Fortune 500 companies on everything from investment to pitch decks. No problem is too big or too small for Johnson and her teams to take on. A burning desire to get things *right* is what inspired Johnson to strike out on her own in the first place. After more than a decade in tech (plus degrees from MIT, Stanford and UCLA), she wanted to cut through the red tape of most offices and work directly on the projects—and problems—she cared about. But when she was a guest on my podcast, she shared that she, too, occasionally got stuck in the mindset of "it has to be perfect." Eventually, she figured out that "you just have to go and give it a try. There's never going to be a perfect time. You can have an idea, and you can put stuff down on paper as much as you want, but until you actually start doing it and start putting it in the world and getting real feedback, you learn by putting the product or service in the world and seeing how the world responds to it. You're going to learn a lot more from that than sitting there, trying to keep thinking over the idea and trying to make the idea better."

Stop Worrying about Your Logo

I'm involved with an amazing company called Beautycounter. It's a skincare and cosmetics brand focused on sustainable, healthy ingredients and products we can actually feel good about putting on our bodies and faces. In 2018 Beautycounter totally revamped their logo and package designs for the second time. For a company that only started in 2013, this change might seem too hasty—weren't people just beginning to recognize the brand? Wouldn't a design change five years after the launch be confusing, both to customers and to the thousands of team members who represent the company?

But when you know, you know. And Gregg

Renfrew, Beautycounter's founder and CEO, knew she wanted the brand to have a new look. The logo and set of accompanying graphic design changes allowed her to showcase the brand's luxe qualities, while recalling its original color scheme and making it easier for customers to sort products by color family. It also opened the door for a revamp of the packaging itself, which is now more closely aligned with the brand's sustainable values.

The relaunch, prominently featuring the new graphics, debuted just as Beautycounter launched their first brick-and-mortar space in SoHo, probably New York City's trendiest neighborhood and the place to be if you're selling chic, good-for-the-planet (and for you) beauty products.

The Beautycounter logo before this change?

It was fine. Good, even. But it wasn't right for the brand's identity as it had evolved, and that's something Renfrew was only able to figure out after she'd already been in business for five years. If she had tried to nail down *the* logo before launching, she might still be working on it.

Or think about our hypothetical cooking app. Imagine the developers, the marketing team and the sales team agonizing over that Mediterranean versus Middle Eastern part of the algorithm. Let's say, after months of hard work, they finally manage to get it right.

Excited to launch their dream project, the team makes the app available for purchase, certain they've worked out every possible bug and every possible user question.

Now imagine that a week later, a user leaves a comment in the App Store, asking why the cooking app doesn't have an option to search for gluten-free dinner ideas.

Ignorance Is Bliss

For many of us, this is going to take some serious retraining of our brains. If you're a smart, successful, accomplished person, you probably got there because you're a perfectionist (or at least a person with perfectionist tendencies). You studied hard in school, you went over your résumé with a fine-tooth comb, you took your first internship so seriously that the company begged you to come back after graduation. Maybe you're even like this in your personal life, too —dinner is always on the table at 6:30, you never forget a birthday and your friends rave about the elegant thank-you notes you send out after every event.

If you're going to get your business off the ground, though, you have to tell your inner perfectionist to *just shut up* sometimes. Tell her that you know you're going to make mistakes and that you know there are future challenges she can't even imagine.

And then? You leap.

Part of defeating perfectionism is learning to trust our own instincts. So often I see founders get stuck on paper, on the part of launching a brand or a business or idea where you try to refine and refine and refine . . . and then refine some more. The only way to get out of this rut is to tap into what you know, think and feel is the right way forward for your business.

Angela Leet is the founder of ALEETCO, a full-service construction management firm. Leet is a certifiably badass CEO. Working in a male-dominated industry that often hews to an old-school way of doing things, she has firsthand experience with questioning her instincts. On my podcast, we talked about what that does to even the most headstrong entrepreneurs:

Angela: "My truth is that sometimes I fear starting because I don't know exactly how I'm going to get there. And so I hold myself back. When in reality, I would have been far better off if I'd followed my instincts. If I'd gone with what my intuition tells me and just done it."

Mimi: "It's like analysis paralysis."

Analysis paralysis is a swamp that traps so many people with perfectionist tendencies. It's easy to think that if a little bit of analysis gets good results, a ton of analysis will get amazing results. But there has to be a middle ground—a space between "doing your homework" and "getting a PhD." A space where you can trust that you've done all you can do, and now it's time to see how your ideas fly.

The lesson here is that you will never be ready—and once you accept that, it can be freeing. You will always be adapting, changing and learning. And isn't that where the best ideas and the most groundbreaking innovations come from? The "it" ideas that take businesses from "pretty good" to "off the charts"?

All that being said, there is absolutely a time for insisting on perfection, especially when high-profile clients or investors are involved. Again, once you've come to understand what your customers consider to be quality, you should always strive to deliver it.

I learned this lesson the hard way. No matter how much time I put into one past project to make it perfect, it just wouldn't be so.

I was working on an initial public offering for an airline company. It was a Friday afternoon at 4:30 pm, and I was finalizing an internal memorandum to send to all the senior executives at the bank to vote on. FedEx was coming at 6 pm to pick up all our documents. As we were stapling these hundreds of sheets of paper together, making the packets that executives would read over the weekend, we found a typo. We had to run to the eighth floor, beg the secretary not to go home and instead fire up an ancient computer, run the spell check again and print out another metric ton of paper. So we were relying completely on someone else—someone else who had less personal stake in the outcome than we did. I made sure the typo was corrected, but I didn't have time to do a full proofread of the document. Still, I was sure this typo was the only mistake that needed fixing, and I was relieved—and more than a little bit proud of my hustle in getting it corrected.

Everything was finally reprinted, and we began frantically stapling all over again to meet the 6 pm deadline. We barely made it, but 20 copies went out via FedEx to the investment committee.

Just as I was catching my breath, excited to put this long day behind me and get my weekend started, the phone rang.

I picked up the phone and heard my boss on the other end, muttering furiously. "*No, no, no,*" he said, followed by the last words you ever want to hear from your boss on a Friday night:

"What the fuck happened?"

My boss was a teddy bear, so I knew from his reaction that I'd made a huge mistake. He was mad. Really mad.

"Sir?" I asked tentatively, anxiously awaiting his response.

It turns out the spell check corrected our typo, but it also autocorrected the last name of a research analyst we cited—over 100 times—from Buttricks to Buttocks.

So, as they say, don't let the perfect be the enemy of the good. And also, *never* trust spell check.

5

WHAT IT REALLY MEANS TO BE CEO

Think back to high school, remember those popularity polls that were the staple of all yearbooks? There was always a category for Most Likely to Succeed. We used our teenage brains to come up with the right answer and a list would form: someone with top grades, a star athlete, a boldly confident student or even sometimes the prettiest student. I would come to find out that neither looks, smarts nor confidence is the key to entrepreneurial successes. The most necessary trait? Adaptability.

When you think about what starting a new business requires of a person, think about Eric Ries's definition for a startup: "A startup is a human institution designed to deliver a new product or service under conditions of extreme uncertainty."

What is going to get you through extreme uncertainty? Adaptability.

When I'm approached about investing in a new company, I need to understand the product first. If it's not ready, or it doesn't do what it tells me it's going to do or I don't believe the market is there, it's a nonstarter.

But if I *do* like the product, the next thing that needs to sell me is the CEO—the person who wants my money to help bring their vision to life.

Especially when companies are just starting out—because in the early days, the CEO *is* the company. They're the person running the show, and one of the first things I look for is their ability to, well, run the show. To prove to me that they own any mistakes or errors, that they have vision, and that they have heart. Here are some things that are nonnegotiable when I'm looking at a CEO and deciding whether or not I want to invest in them:

- If you're the CEO, the buck stops with you. I need to know that you're ready to take full responsibility for everything that goes out the door. And that doesn't mean I need everything that goes out the door to be perfect—we're all human, and a typo in a printed memo isn't the end of the world. But I want to see you acknowledge those typos and not to pass the blame—if you blame your secretary (or worse, berate her in front of me), I'll see a CEO who isn't ready to shoulder the responsibility of a thriving brand.

- I want CEOs I work with to be invested— with money, time or energy of their own (and ideally, I'd like to see all three). That shows me that you're just as in this as you want me to be.

- Can you solve problems? If something goes wrong, can you pivot? Or do you get flustered, stuck and insistent that what you did should have worked? Even the most successful, most well-run businesses face crises, whether it's a phone bill someone forgot to pay or an ingredient that compromises the integrity of your formula. I want to see that when the going gets tough, you, the captain of this ship, get even tougher.

- Are you going it alone? If so, that's a red flag. We'll talk more about building a team in the next chapter, but I need to see that a founder knows when it's time to bring in outside help, and that they know how to do that in a way that makes sense for their brand.

I've interviewed a ton of amazing female CEOs on my podcast. They all have different stories, different ideas, different work styles and different dreams. But after doing the show for the past year, I quickly noticed that all of these badass founders shared some innate qualities and that by listening to their stories, we get the chance to look for those things within ourselves.

So here are the questions I'd advise any aspiring CEO to ask of herself:

Are you optimistic?

If you've been paying attention to market trends over the last few years, you'll know that cannabis-based products—from snacks to drinks to lotions to pet treatments—are incredibly hot. Marijuana-based goods have gone mainstream, and you're just as likely to find an elegant CBD-infused tea in the refrigerator of an upscale home as you are a bottle of Pinot Grigio.

Hilary McCain is the founder of Sweet Reason beverages, a line of cannabis- and hemp-infused drinks with flavors like strawberry lavender and lemon rhubarb. In their chic bottles, Sweet Reason drinks offer consumers a natural way to unwind and recharge, and the brand prides itself on using high-quality ingredients (not to mention the fact that a portion of every sale goes to mental health research charities).

When I spoke with McCain, she told me that the key to an entrepreneur's success lies in a firm commitment to optimism.

"[A sense of optimism] is just so important in the ability to survive entrepreneurship...to really look at problems optimistically and know that there is a solution to everything, that they just have to find it. And that they are able to solve it, even if they've never done it before." It's not about being in a good mood all the time, or about refusing to engage with challenges or negative feedback. It's a firm belief that what you're doing is the right thing and that you are the right—and the only—person who can do it.

Are you committed to lifelong learning?

I couldn't wait to graduate from business school. Finally my education would be finished, I thought, and it would be time to leap into the world of entrepreneurship. I was ready to apply everything I'd learned to my future empire.

And I spent a *lot* of time in school, as most of us do.

But if the day you graduate is the day you think you're done with learning, you couldn't be more wrong. I've said that a good CEO knows when she needs to know more, and in the case of many great brands, it's that hunger for knowledge that leads to the million-dollar idea.

Whatever your field, whatever your interests—do you want to know more? Are you willing to be taught? Even if you're already an expert, are you willing to admit you still have a lot to learn?

"There are successful entrepreneurs who didn't even go to college, and who certainly don't have business backgrounds. So I really think it comes down to the person, whether or not they can figure it out," Kiri Cole Popa of The Health Examiner (more on her later!) once told me.

I love this take, because it demonstrates something I think is really important to remember about becoming a CEO: it's really and truly never too late. All those "30 Under 30" lists? Stories about wunderkind founders who sell their first apps to Google straight out of Harvard?

Ignore them. You don't have to know you want to be a CEO from the day you start third grade, and you certainly don't have to know you want to be a CEO the day you finish school, whether it's after your senior year of high school or ten years into a postgraduate degree. A passion for learning—for wanting to know where, when, why and how—is *way* more impressive to a smart investor than the names on your résumé.

Learning, of course, leads to doing, which brings us to the next question I want you to consider.

Are you open to failure?

A good CEO is one who fails—ideally, one who fails often!

That might sound counterintuitive, especially if you're constantly bombarded with stories of successful people who take one idea, spin it into a billion dollars and then tell you that making it to the top is easy.

But for every great idea, or great success, there are ten ideas that, well...aren't so great. Or 10 new visions for how to run a business that sound great on paper but flop in the real world.

When we dug into the narratives about failure, Suze Schwartz said: "You're going to fail. And failure is just a way to get better...Not everybody starts and is crushing it from day one! And most of the entrepreneur stories you'll hear are people who started and got crushed, and then they crushed it."

In many ways, your first big failure should be a

relief. You've gotten over it, and you're still here! You've proved to yourself—and your investors, not to mention your employees, friends and family—that you have the ability to get back up after a fall.

Casey Georgeson's Saint Jane Beauty is an ultra-luxe skincare line that utilizes CBD in its moisturizers and serums. Georgeson was the first person to take CBD products to the high-end market, and when you're the first, you're inevitably going to strike out from time to time. But what Georgeson told me on the podcast is that the failures themselves don't matter—it's what happens next.

"Just go easy on yourself, because it's a learning process, and you're going to have tons of failures," she said. "You're going to have wins, hopefully that balance out the failures. But the failures are tough, and you have to pick stuff up and move on quickly and not let it go too deep—because there's so much ahead!"

Are you (a little) crazy?

If I had wanted it, I could have stayed in finance. I could have stayed in accounting. And I could have stayed at Bloomingdale's.

When I quit each of those jobs, I'm sure plenty of people in my life thought I was crazy. I was giving up good salaries, good career paths and associations with extremely prestigious companies. What more could I want?

The truth is, I am a little crazy. Because entrepreneurship is in my blood, and I believe wholeheartedly that every true entrepreneur is a little nuts.

Georgeson's career arc looked pretty similar to mine. She had degrees from great schools and jobs at companies like CNN and Sephora. If she'd wanted to, she could probably be *president* of CNN or Sephora. But she knew she was meant to blaze her own trail.

"You have to be a little crazy," she told me. "You have to be willing to put in the work, and you have to be kind of addicted to it. It's not a decision right now. I just am so compelled to do it. And I think that's what I didn't expect." When she started Saint Jane, she knew she had to go all-in, which requires a kind of willing suspension of disbelief. You have to believe that people will want your product, you have to believe that the money will come when you need it, and you have to believe that you're going to get it right. Carly Stein, founder of Beekeeper's Naturals, said something similar when she was on my podcast. When she told people she wanted to leave her job as a financial analyst at Goldman Sachs to focus on her brand of all-natural alternatives to traditional OTC medicines, people thought she was nuts—why give up such a prestigious (and lucrative) career. But Stein believed in her vision and was eventually able to get her product into Whole Foods, where today it's a bestseller in their booming natural remedies division.

The lesson is: if people think you sound crazy? You're on the right track.

Are you adaptable?

It's important to have convictions, values and boundaries. If you don't have those things and really root yourself and your work in them, there's only so far you can go.

But just like the tall buildings designed to gently sway with earthquakes and hurricanes rather than break apart, you've also got to be adaptable.

Think of it this way: most of us have relationships with a wide variety of people. You might have parents, a spouse, kids, friends, employees, bosses, acquaintances, even frenemies. Would you interact with all of these people in exactly the same way? Would it make sense to talk to your boss the way you'd talk to your husband, or to your kids the way you'd talk to your best girlfriends?

Of course not. You're still you during all of these

interactions, but you're a *you* who adapts to different people and different situations. It's key that any CEO brings that kind of flexibility to work because work is *filled* with people who have different wants, needs, goals and communication styles.

Working in construction management, Angela Leet has had to deal with a wide variety of personalities—sometimes on the same job sites.

"There are times when I've learned to use being a female in a male industry to my advantage...If I have to be sweet to somebody, I can pour on sweet. I can pour on bitch...I can wear my yoga pants or I can wear my cowboy outfit or I can wear my formal gown. Whatever the event is, I can show up prepared in the right outfit," she told me.

And the idea of wearing the right outfit is a great metaphor. So often our vision of the founder is Steve Jobs in his signature turtleneck, or Mark Zuckerberg in the same gray T-shirt and hoodie. But don't you want to be a founder who uses every color of the rainbow? One who knows when it's time to put on the ball gown or the cowboy boots?

When I'm looking to invest, my interest is always piqued by founders who can do it all, who seem as comfortable in the boardroom as they are jumping in to teach a yoga class when an instructor calls in sick. If you show people that you, too, can be flexible, it will be easy for them to envision you as the kind of CEO who can take whatever gets thrown at you.

Are you patient?

You might not be as excited about this question.

After all, who likes waiting? I'm guilty of this myself—when you're an ideas person, it's easy to get swept away by thinking of a future in which your idea has debuted to tons of fanfare. How many founders have come up with a great product and instantly envisioned it on the cover of a magazine (or those same magazines doing cover stories on *them* and their runaway smash hit)? There's a huge gulf between the idea and the Forbes 500, though, and if you focus too much on the latter you run the real risk of not even getting off the ground.

"I think patience is probably number one," said Tara Dowburd, founder of the uber-busy and in-demand Make Up Therapy, a glam squad based out of Los Angeles. "You really have to be patient because to really build a great business, it doesn't happen overnight."

I've seen so many founders, many of whom were incredibly smart and talented, flame out. Maybe they launched too soon, scaled too fast or shared details about proprietary ideas before they were fully sketched out. And I know it's tempting to shout everything from the rooftops, especially in an age when so many of us use social media to communicate and to crowd-source feedback.

But just like Dowburd said: a great business doesn't happen overnight, and anyone who tells you otherwise isn't telling you the whole story. Same goes for anyone who tells you it's easy: I can count on one hand the number of times I've truly taken a day off, and owning your own business also means being constantly available. It might mean working tirelessly after the kids are in bed or ordering takeout instead of cooking so you can prep for a big presentation. But in the end, this work is the work you have to do, especially when you're just starting out.

There's an old canard: you only get one chance to make a first impression. So why not slow down and make it count, knowing you've worked your butt off to make it the best first impression it can be?

Here's a final question I want you to be thinking about. It's a little harder to quantify, but it's maybe the most important question we'll ask in this book.

Do you have chutzpah?

You might know this Yiddish term by another word: *moxie*. Or in Spanish: *cojones*.

Do you have the guts, the gall, the audacity to take your shot?

A good idea and a tightly knit team are important, but it's mostly about the chutzpah. It's an ineffable quality that demonstrates that you've got the right combination of strength, skills, drive and heart to jump off the cliff and into the ocean of your future. I talked about chutzpah with Victoria Montgomery Brown, cofounder and CEO of leading digital media knowledge company BigThink, and she said something that I think really cuts to the center of what makes this quality so important. "To be a successful entrepreneur takes a great idea, the understanding that there's a market for it, that you've researched, that is differentiated, that you and your partners...are uniquely positioned to build the business. And then, going for it. I just think it's mostly about chutzpah and taking the leap."

It's about saying to yourself: I've done my due diligence and put my sweat equity into this project. I've done my homework and checked it twice.

It's time to go for it.

I also want to share a story Angela Leet told me about those pivotal moments in which we discover the chutzpah we didn't even know we had:

"I had a subcontractor who was out working on an old pipeline. It had asbestos on it. They were responsible for removing the pipeline and putting a new pipeline in, and they weren't following the procedures that needed to be done. So I went out there to basically say, 'Here's the things that we need to do to make sure that we're complying with the laws.'"

And I remember him patting me on my hard hat and saying 'Look, missy, we've got this under control.'

And you either say, 'All right, this guy is scaring the shit out of me.'

Or you say, 'You know what? I know what I'm doing. And I'm going to tell you how this is actually going to happen.'

And that's what I did. I stood up to him. And I probably hadn't been on the job more than three months at this point. And I said, 'Well, sir, let me tell you actually how this is going to happen. I hold your work permit. And if you want to continue to have your crew out here today, you're going to follow our rules.'

And his tone completely changed. And then we had to have a discussion because he realized, 'Wait a minute, she could kick me off the job site. And then I don't get to pay my guys today. I might lose the job because I get behind on the schedule.' Now he had to make a choice, too. He was either going to actually attempt to have a conversation and we were going to come up with a compromise that worked, that met everybody's criteria; or instead of being a badass, he was going to be a jackass and he was going to have to kick his crew out. For me, it kind of set a tone in my career."

When celebrity chef Giada De Laurentiis was preparing to open her first restaurant in Las Vegas, there was a team of restaurant veterans and businessmen ready to tell her how things had always been done.

But De Laurentiis hadn't gotten to where she was by doing things the way they'd always been done, and her vision for this restaurant, too, was her own.

"I wanted these five windows that open up so that you feel suspended over the Strip, and you could actually feel the Bellagio fountains—so it felt like you were literally suspended over them," she told me on my podcast.

But no one had pulled off that kind of design before, and the team was hesitant.

"And at the end of the day," De Laurentiis continued, "I just got up and I said, 'If you don't give me the windows, then I will sue you and I will get out of this contract. I will not open this place without these windows.'"

And De Laurentiis's windows? She got them.

And that, to me, is the beauty of chutzpah. It's not about walking around strutting your stuff 24/7, acting like the toughest kid on the playground.

It's about knowing your power—and not being afraid to use it.

6

BUILDING A TEAM: HOW TO DEFINE ROLES—AND RELATIONSHIPS

One night I found myself crouched over an embroidery machine with bobbins and streams of measuring tape scattered around me. My fingers were throbbing from trying to get the cursive slant *just right* on the name "DANIEL" across the two-inch pocket of a baby onesie. *God,* I thought to myself, *what a waste of my MBA.* I had started my own monogramming business for baby clothes. Monogramming has been around for decades, but it was typically found on linens in upscale department stores, or in mall shops that embroider baseball hats and jerseys—not places a new mom would typically go for baby clothes. This was years before the posh monogram shops showed up in trendy shopping districts on the Upper East Side and in Beverly Hills or Mark and Graham existed.

To launch my monogramming business, I set up booths at holiday fairs, Mother's Day events, and maternity conventions. I'd monogram items for my friends who I knew had a big network of friends having babies. From these grassroots sales, I started getting a flood of new orders for baby gifts. Every baby gift led to more baby gifts. Remember, I had no social media at this point. I didn't even need to pay for advertising—it was all happening via word of mouth. It turned out there was a huge demand for elegantly monogrammed baby clothes. My biggest mistake? Once I was doing six figures and had over 200 orders, I still thought I could run this business by myself. But I quickly burnt out and sold my embroidery machine. In the years since, I've watched the personal monogram market explode. Just think: I could have been Mark and Graham.

Now, years later, I can look at the whole thing with a clear head and sharp eyes.

So here are some of the things I could have done. I could have gone to friends and family with a business plan and asked them to invest so I could finance more staff or an outsourcing operation. There are also plenty of overseas garment operations that have whole factory floors of workers at embroidery machines. Or I could have struck a deal with an established embroidery operation and handed over my metric ton of onesies and baby towels. Or I could have reached out for financing to start my own brick-and-mortar store or catalog. Yet despite my success and proof of concept, I didn't have the confidence to reach out.

That experience taught me a lot—as every failure should. My expertise is not in the fine art of stitching or hand lettering (though I am actually pretty good at both of those things). My expertise is in spotting inefficiencies and holes in the market and then working with innovators to plug them. As mergers and acquisitions expert Michelle Seiler Tucker told me during our podcast interview, "You have to focus on your strengths and hire your weaknesses." Tucker is a leading authority on buying, selling, fixing and growing businesses and coauthor of *Exit Rich*. "So many entrepreneurs make the mistake of trying to do everything themselves," she added, "and that's a big mistake. If your idea is as good as you think it is, then you'll be able to find the financing to outsource pain points, and you'll be able to find smart, talented, driven people who want to be on your team."

Alana Ruoso, a success and personal development coach for creatives and designers, echoed Tucker's point: "So many women are overachievers," she opined. "You just hold on to everything because you want to control it. You want to be responsible for the success of all of it."

When you try to do everything yourself, you are perpetuating your own struggle. Sadly, that struggle can become an almost addictive cycle for some. Ruoso went on to say, "The more we let go, the more we end up releasing struggle."

You need to be aware of what makes you feel overwhelmed and stressed. Take a hard look at your calendar and examine what is necessary for you to do and what you are able to delegate to others (or allow others to have ownership of) or let go of altogether. Don't perpetuate your own struggle.

When I see a driven, hyperfocused entrepreneur who is doing it all, I see a red flag. I see someone who is too controlling to acknowledge their own strengths and weaknesses.

I know that when you work on something every night after work, during every stolen minute of a busy weekend while the kids are napping and the laundry is drying, it can be hard to let go or to let other people in. Trusting that other people are going to do the right thing with your brand is scary.

You may already have a team, or you may be doing this solo. As an investor I want to share with you what I see as ideal (and less than ideal) teams that influence my willingness to fund a new company.

How does partnership impact growth?

Fifty-fifty arrangements that typically start off with so much starry-eyed enthusiasm and passion tend to unravel into a chaotic mess full of hurt feelings, recriminations and lawsuits (especially when it's two *friends* who decided to split things right down the middle). Friends who become business partners often do so because they have similar motivations, talents and values. But similar doesn't translate into success. A good business partner has opposing talents. I feel more confident investing in a partnership that's codified by complementary strengths and weaknesses rather than by two friends who vacation together. While you may think partnering with your like-minded friend is doubling your strengths, if you're too similar, you're also doubling your weaknesses.

If you are unable to look your partner in the eye and candidly answer these two questions, then you should not go into business together:

- What is your single most important behavioral quality that contributes to the strength of the business?
- What is your single most important behavioral quality that detracts from the strength of the team?

That being said, we often need a partner to dream big with, so if you and your bestie happened to come up with, say, the best way to disrupt the leisurewear industry while on vacation in Cabo, then take an honest inventory of the partnership and put it in writing.

Next step: talk about what you want your work lives to look and feel like. Just like we did in chapter 1, conceptualize your fantasy work life together (you can flip to the back of the book to a useful list of questions to ask each other). While you guys start this business together, what do weekends look like? Are you going to answer emails then? Are you going to stay home to work on a deck for your business plan? If one of you bolts awake with an idea at 2 am, is it okay to call? There's no right answer to these questions, but they can be wildly different—which is where you're going to run into big problems. It's not just about respecting one another's boundaries; it's also about collaborating effectively.

Maybe you find weekends to be the ideal time to get the most work done. Or maybe you work tirelessly all week bootstrapping a company, keeping your family at arm's length until you get to the weekend and then turn your phone off so you can be completely present with your kids. Or maybe your work and family life overlap much more, and you spend weekdays supporting the kids' schoolwork (and their hobbies, parties and whims), taking calls between stops but not responding to emails until 1 am. Other days, you spend six hours straight deeply focused on a work project and forget to eat. I know that I require flexibility from a business partner, whereas others require routine. Maybe you can still partner with a friend who doesn't work weekends or odd hours, but does that mean it's fair to do a 50/50 split?

Most importantly, ask: who makes the final decision if you don't agree? This is why it is important to not have a 50/50 split. There needs to be one partner with a slightly higher percentage who will have the final say when a disagreement occurs.

While it's easy to get intoxicated on your shared ambitions and schemes to take the world by storm, you also need to embrace the unsexy part of partnership: analyzing your goals, roles, process and interpersonal dynamics. This is part of a four-step project planning tool developed by organizational theorist Richard Beckhard to help team leaders ensure productivity, efficiency and quality. To summarize Beckhard:

- Goals are what you agree and commit to accomplishing.
- Your roles are clearly defined and free of overlap or conflict.

- Process refers to the methods you'll use to problem solve, innovate, allocate resources, communicate and make decisions.
- Examine communication styles, trust and conflict resolution.

How do you deal with conflict? Do you embrace it? Do you run from it?

If all of these criteria are clearly defined and agreed to, then your interpersonal drama should be minimal. If you're already experiencing some friction with a friend/business partner, and you think it's because you have opposing star signs or because one of you still hasn't gotten over a snide remark made at a dinner party five years ago, I encourage you to assess whether the root of your problem doesn't have to do with ill-defined goals, roles or process. You can flip to the back to go through a goals, roles and process checklist.

Once that's all sorted out, the next step is to put this in writing and be prepared to share it.

It can be tempting to form a 50/50 partnership, especially if you feel like the other person can bring something you can't. In my experience, this rarely works. Someone has to be responsible for making decisions. There are some instances in which a company will have two people who occupy the founder/CEO slot, usually when it's a joint project or idea from the inception. When that happens, consider adopting a framework like the Goals, Roles, Processes and Interpersonal Relationships (GRPI) model. Developed in the 1970s by an organizational theorist, it's a system designed to help teams streamline decision-making processes and avoid getting stuck in endless cycles of dysfunction.

Follow the Money

Sometimes you have a buddy with a lot of money and a lot of faith in your idea. That's fantastic. But if they are part of your business plan, then they better have some bona fides besides disposable cash. If I see a name in your business plan, look it up and don't find a LinkedIn profile but instead just an Instagram with sleazy photos full of bottle service, it's a hard pass. Also, as conventional wisdom goes, the earlier the hire, the bigger the impact on the company. So imagine the impact of a founder with a reputation that's just a big question mark. If this person does not have functionality beyond their willingness to spend money, then they will be dead weight and a drain on your cap table.

Beware of any money that seems too good to be true. There are a lot of would-be investors out there, and most of the time that's a huge plus when trying to start a new business. After all, you never know where funding might come from, and it's exciting to think of making connections in unexpected places. But not all money is created equal. If you're at the point where you're ready to take on outside funding, either through a formal partnership or something like a silent partnership, you have to be choosy about whose cash you accept. Does your investor have the same values as you? Do they share your vision for your company's future? Are they someone you'd trust, or feel comfortable recommending to someone else? If you're not sure about the answers to any of these questions, it might be smart to move on.

Titles Have to Mean Something

Titles are only as useful as the person behind them. I've seen fledgling companies make the mistake of giving people the title of COO or a cofounder credit to an executive brought on early just because it sounds good. It is almost always a mistake. Executives serve a very specific purpose and carry a great deal of responsibility; it benefits nobody to give people titles they haven't earned. It's also not beneficial to give an executive you hired a cofounder designation just because it sounds good. Titles don't make the woman—the woman makes the title, so to speak. Someone at an executive level has to have earned their stripes, and there's nothing wrong with bringing on an executive team from outside of your organization. Realizing that your founding team can't be experts in all areas is a key element to success and growth. You also don't need to credit someone as a cofounder just because you hired them early on. If you're working with people who are focused on what they can put on their business card (whether they've earned it or not), you're working with the wrong people.

If you're going to make someone a cofounder, do so because they were instrumental in bringing the business together. This doesn't mean they need to have incredible technical expertise or a funding stream.

The subject of team building comes up a lot on my podcast. So many of the women I interview started with an idea and fine-tuned it in their kitchens or living rooms, soliciting feedback from immediate family and close friends before launching. Since so many of the women I interview are smart, successful businesswomen, they started small, growing in a way that they could actually manage. When it came time to start hiring team members, a lot of them were—understandably—freaked out. When you're dealing with money and ideas, there's so much advice out there centered on how to hire and how to expand, and a lot of it conflicts. Should you hire friends? Should you avoid hiring friends? Should you hire for skills? Experience?

Personality? The answers to these questions might look different for everyone, but I'd like to share a few pieces of hard-won wisdom from some of my favorite guests.

The Trial Period

Many major companies structure new hire contracts in a way that makes the first 30 or 60 days of employment a trial period, where new hires are getting paid and onboarded, but you, the boss, reserve the right to end the relationship if things aren't working out. You're not a major company (yet), but you should do the same thing. In the early stages of development, each hire you make is crucial. A mismatch in a position like sales manager, accountant or production designer could cost you literal years of progress and tons of money. So start slow: consider hiring someone to work for you part-time until you both get a sense for how good a fit the relationship is.

Or why not outsource and work with consultants when you're just getting off the ground? Outsourcing enables you to work with a wide variety of people and to get only the work you need without having to navigate official hiring (and firing).

It's also important to use this time to make sure people you're bringing onto your team work well with the people who are already there. And listen, we're talking about a business here, not a slumber party. The people on your team don't need to get along like life-long friends. But they do need to bring out the best in each other when it comes to achieving goals, which is why you should solicit opinions and feedback from your existing employees about new hires, both formally and informally.

And when you first start hiring? That's a trial period for you, too. If you've been doing it all on your own, delegating is going to take some getting used to—but it's essential. "I think making wise decisions on where to involve yourself or where to transfer owner-ship and responsibilities, is really important as well," said Vera Koch, VP of global marketing for custom hair color brands eSalon and Colorsmith, when I spoke to her on my podcast. "To manage your own time wisely. I think that that's also been helpful for me to always challenge myself to say, should I be participating in this meeting? Should I be delegating this task? Or do I need to be involved? Yet at the same time, for my team to know [that] when you need me, I'll be there for you."

You should use your own trial period to practice letting other people handle things, have meetings and get things done without you watching. It's good practice for the eventual moment in which you won't have time to be hands-on in every single aspect of business. It's also the only way to really determine whether the people you've chosen to become part of your team are the right ones for the job. "If you don't hire the right people, you will not succeed," Brooke Mason told me when we talked about this on the podcast. "You have to have those right people. Take your time with it. Be very precise with it."

Be Honest about Your Environment

It can be hard to be objective about our own working styles. One woman's fast-paced, rapid-fire office might be a total nightmare for someone who likes to take plenty of time to ponder each step. When you're building a team, you want to look for people who will thrive under your leadership, and that starts with identifying what your leadership style actually looks like.

My favorite bosses were the ones who gave me long leashes. I hate being micromanaged, and I learn best—and work smartest—when I have the opportunity to really take ownership over my work. To make mistakes and learn the *hows* and *whys*, not just be told that I'm wrong. If I'm hiring, I want people to know that this is the sort kind of environment I cultivate as a boss. I want employees who take initiative and learn by doing, rather than ones who will need to ask me a million questions just to make sure they're getting everything right from the get-go.

That's just my style. Other people like to micro-manage, and plenty of employees thrive in the sort of environment where there's close supervision and hand-holding. The important thing isn't to totally change your company's environment, or the style of your leadership, but to be honest about what those things actually look like.

When you're hiring, let potential employees tell you about *their* ideal workplaces, too. On the very first episode of my podcast, I sat down with Tara Dowburd, a makeup artist with nearly two decades of experience styling women for weddings and high-profile events. Her work has been featured in *Vogue*, *Glamour* and *Martha Stewart Weddings*, and in 2008 she took her training—which included work at Neiman Marcus, Bloomingdale's and a degree in fashion marketing— and started Make-Up Therapy, a full-service company that now employs nearly 20 makeup artists and hair-stylists who work on projects all over California.

After years of doing everything from the booking to the advertising to the eyeliner application herself, Tara knew she was going to have to hire if she was going to expand. And her strategy for finding the right people was simple. "I would meet with [a potential team member] and talk to them versus me just jumping in and telling them everything," she said. "I would really just listen about what they were about and their style and their aesthetic and the way they work and timing and all that. And when I listened to that, I didn't have to tell them really what I was looking for. They were telling me."

A job interview is a two-way street: you're trying to figure out if this candidate is the best person for the job, but they're also trying to figure out whether or not your company is a good fit for them. The more you can be honest about your office and its culture—and let prospective employees be honest about their likes, dislikes, strengths and weaknesses—the stronger your team will be.

Hire for Your Weaknesses

A mistake I see a lot of founders make when it comes to hiring is this: they're smart, driven, Type-A, super-organized workaholics. And so when it's time to look for employees, they look for people who are... smart, driven, Type-A, super-organized workaholics. Younger versions of themselves, maybe, or people who finish their sentences during every brainstorming meeting.

And while there's something to be said for having a team that understands your vision and your values, it's also important to remember that nobody—no founder—is perfect. Building a team is an opportunity to get closer to perfection than you would alone, because it's your chance to think about all the things you're not so great at and *hire people who are actually great at them*.

As Michelle Seiler Tucker put it on my podcast: "I think most entrepreneurs are probably not good people managers at all, because we're entrepreneurs, we expect everybody to be like us." When you can be honest about your own limitations, you can begin to build a team designed to overcome them.

Kiri Cole Popa is the founder, CEO and publisher of The Health Examiner, a great website that makes it easy for the average person to learn about holistic wellness and natural medicine. When she was a guest on my podcast, Popa told me that she knew she was the person to launch this business successfully: in addition to having an MBA from Duke, she's also a certified wellness coach who works with individuals and practitioners looking to expand their reach.

What she didn't know how to do was build websites.

"As an entrepreneur, you have to hire people in areas of your business where you may not really have expertise or connections," she told me. "For example, I needed a competent website developer to build a site that I envisioned. I have limited knowledge in technology and few contacts. So finding that right person was a challenge. And this is where you really have to hustle unless you are wealthy and very well connected. Some people are, but many aren't. Hustling naturally comes with the territory when you're an entrepreneur...You've got to comb through your contacts...network constantly [and] learn as much as you can to get the people you need and to make the helpful connection."

If Popa had been reluctant to hire someone to build the site for her, where would her business be now? Sure, there are plenty of online platforms that make it easy to host and design your own site. But do they have the functionality that makes The Health Examiner so successful? The design options, the hosting capabilities? By looking for people who knew what she didn't, Popa was able to make her brand stronger when it counted, which in turn made it easier for her to gain followers, attract attention and expand her reach.

It's not just hard skills you should be thinking about here, either. A variety of viewpoints, life experiences and thought styles will make your business stronger because you'll be surrounded by people who ask questions that allow you, as the founder and CEO, to make better decisions. Even something like a simple personality test can help you build your own dream team—an INTJ and an ENFP, both personality types outlined by the famous Myers-Briggs test, will approach a problem with totally different solutions. Of course, no online personality test can tell you exactly what a potential employee will be like to work with, but it's a great way to dig into someone's "why." Why do they want to work for you? What sort of work do they see themselves doing? Why do they get up in the morning? How do they see themselves? A good applicant will be able to rattle off answers to these questions on command, but are those their real answers? Maybe. Taking a personality test and discussing the results is a great way to have more candid conversation about what your potential hire's real ambitions are and how they align with yours.

I want to share a final thought on hiring, which will bring us back to the idea that as the founder, one of the most important tools you have is your own power of discernment.

When Stefanie Cove, the founder of global event design and production company Stefanie Cove and Company, is hiring, she's looking for a person she knows will slot seamlessly into her company. Finding The One isn't always easy.

"The hardest part of our job is finding good people," she told me. "I think that my process is a little nonconventional. Obviously when they first come in, I still feel like I can tell from my gut if someone's going to fit in and be able to work with us. Our pace is super fast. We work all the time. I like people to respond to emails almost immediately because it feels like that's what keeps everyone very calm...I also want to know what kind of a person they are. And I think that is really more important than what their experience is or how much they know about lighting and sound. Because if they're not a kind, thoughtful soul that really wants to take care of others, it's probably not going to be the position for them. In the end, I really like to rely on my gut."

There's a common saying: hire slow, fire fast. That doesn't mean you should drag your feet forever when hiring, and it also doesn't mean you should let someone go for using the wrong kind of pen. But it does mean you should take your time when putting your team together, and it also means that if someone isn't working out, you shouldn't be afraid to end the relationship.

I also think you have to look at more than a person's résumé. Michelle Seiler Tucker agrees: "You really have to look at each role and rate that role with what's the most important thing. Is the most important thing dependability? Punctuality? Loyalty? Is it attention to detail? Is it they've got to be extremely intelligent in this area?" Those are things that job history might not tell you, so Tucker likes to use personality tests (a move

Brooke Harris of Goodmylk, who we'll chat about more in a bit, also employs).

When you're hiring someone, it's because *you're* in charge. Own that power, use it and watch your business flourish.

7

TO FUND OR NOT TO FUND

If you're interested in business in 2021, there are some terms you probably hear a *lot*:

VC. Angel investors. Friends and family money. Series A, Series B and Series C. IPO.

It seems like when it comes to money and business, everyone's an expert. But what you're an expert on is your own business, and these terms are meaningful because they carry serious weight when it comes to your company's future.

Even if your idea is still a daydream, and even if you haven't even *thought* of your big idea yet, this chapter will prepare you to answer the age-old question about life-changing (and world-changing) ideas: *How are you going to pay for it?*

Knowing when to seek outside funding is tricky— you don't want to do it when you're too small. If you raise a bunch of money and don't know how to spend it, you might find yourself having used up the goodwill of the people who know you. You could also find yourself in the position of having taken too much money and given up too much equity too early in the life of your company. That means it's important to think carefully—and honestly—about when your brand is ready for an infusion of cash.

When you're ready to move forward, the next thing you'll likely do is try to secure what's called *friends and family money*. It's pretty self-explanatory: this is money that comes from people who know you and your product, and it's usually earmarked for a specific purpose—for example, to purchase equipment or pay a website designer.

If that goes well, and you've started to develop an established brand and a foothold in your target market, it might be time to look for an angel investor, which is a person who provides funding for an emerging business, usually in exchange for equity in the company. Many angel investors operate independently of venture capital or other kinds of investment firms. An angel investor might be someone in your network (or in your extended network) or a thought leader in your field who thinks .your brand has real potential. Tegan Bukowski is the founder of WellSet, a platform that lets customers and patients book appointments with thousands of natural health practitioners and healers. When looking for an angel investor, she explained on my podcast, "You have to prove that you have an interested base of clients or users, and also maybe even have a product at this point, in order to get funding. That all has to happen while you're still covering your finances."

That last part is key—I want to see that you're a responsible spender and that your business model is sustainable, even if you're not 100 percent there yet. If your product is too expensive to make, for example, it's not going to be a worthwhile investment for me *or* for you.

So what else do angel investors look for? Lucky for you, I *am* one, so I'm going to tell you.

When I'm looking at a company I might want to invest in, I'm not necessarily looking for a company that's bringing in tons of money, at least not in its early stages. What I want to see is that you can sell me—and your customers—the dream of your product, the size of your market and your potential for growth

I also want to know exactly how you'd use my money. I would rather know, for example, that my money is being spent on a marketing plan or an inventory—something to generate customers or income—instead of making the CEO's safety net bigger, or to pay for fancy office space or splashy, stunt-based advertising.

In other words, I need to trust you. We're talking about my money and my reputation. That means you have to be up-front with me about *everything*. "The number one piece of advice [for communicating with investors] is transparency at all costs," BigThink's Victoria Montgomery Brown told me. "So for me, it's been really important to deliver the bad news as quickly and as harshly as possible because these people, your investors, have invested in you. And if you lose their confidence or trust, I would say it's virtually impossible to get it back."

I agree: if you're honest with me about problems, I'm probably going to want to work with you to find a solution. But if you're not, how can I know you'll be the kind of business partner I can depend on?

Part of the reason I spend so much time talking about the qualities of a good CEO is because I know firsthand how much those qualities matter to angel investors. I know that if you're not prepared, if you haven't done your research, and if you're unable to successfully execute your concept, it doesn't matter how good the concept itself is—it's just not going to work.

The next chunk of money many companies look to get is what's called "VC money"—VC is short for "venture capital." It's usually a lot more than you'll get from an angel investor, and it comes from a different kind of source—an investment firm, a bank or another corporate entity that sees a future in your product.

"Okay," you're probably thinking right now, "sounds great—where do I sign up to get some of this VC funding?"

Not so fast.

For lots of people, VC money is truly game changing: think about what companies like Uber and Etsy have done with large amounts of cash from high-level Silicon Valley experts. But if you're not careful, VC money can actually hurt your company more than it helps. You have to understand what investors are looking for and what taking their money means for you and your business.

I want to demystify the VC process with the help of Jesse Draper, who was a guest on my podcast last year. Draper is the founding partner of Halogen Ventures, a venture capital firm that specializes in investing in women-led companies. That in and of itself is a rarity, since, as I mentioned before, only 10 percent of VC partners are women, and only 3 percent of women-led companies get VC money. Among the brands in Jesse's portfolio are some you've definitely heard of: female-centric news platform the Skimm, plus-size clothing brand Eloquii and upscale candy retailer Sugarfina. She's appeared on countless TV shows and podcasts, and she's also someone who was born into the business world—Draper is a fourth-generation venture capitalist, and she grew up in the heart of Silicon Valley.

The first thing you have to keep in mind when it comes to taking VC money is that on some level it's like cutting off your big toe and giving it to someone else (who may or may not eventually want your *other* big toe).

"What you should think about as a founder is you're always trying to push up the valuation," says Draper.

Valuation, or how much your company is worth, is based on a variety of factors: a history of your sales, the demonstrated attraction of your product or service to your customer base, what milestones you have hit and what milestones you project to hit next and how these milestones project your future valuation in two, five and even 10 years down the line. The marketplace will also come into play here—if you're at the start of a trend, your valuation might be different than it would be a year into the trend or at the trend's peak.

"And then," Draper continued, "the venture capitalist is always trying to push *down* the valuation. And so you want the biggest valuation you can get, and then the venture capitalist wants the lowest valuation, so they can own the biggest piece of the company. You don't want to give away too much of your company in the beginning, which is what would happen with a very, very low valuation."

In plain terms, that means you want your company to be as valuable as it can be, since it's yours. Venture capitalists want the opposite because what *they* want is to own as much of your company as they can.

"So," Draper added, "you also have to take into account how much money you need and how much you're raising." If someone is throwing millions of dollars at you, it can be tempting to say yes—after all, it's millions of dollars! But slow down. Think about how much money you need versus how much money it might be nice to have. Think about where you'll spend the money itself. And since we've spent so much time talking about the importance of this kind of planning, it should be easy.

It's sort of like getting a haircut: you can always cut more off, but once it's cut, there's no putting it back on. You can always try to raise more money, especially if your business is successful. But whatever money you take from investors is money you can't untake.

So what does Draper look for when she's evaluating a new company?

"Founder, product, traction," she says. To break it down further: a founder who is able to pivot and work with curveballs, a product that is absolutely unique and traction demonstrated via a variety of data points—revenue or a user base if your product already exists, or data proving that the customer base is there. Basically, anything that demonstrates that there is need and opportunity.

She's investing, then, in three things:

You, as the founder and CEO

Your product

Your product's future on the open market

And while Draper only works with whip-smart founders, she knows they can come from anywhere. "I think anyone can start a company! I think some of the best companies in the world have been started by college dropouts, or high school dropouts even. I definitely don't care where you came from or what your background is, I just care that you are building something incredible, and that you're excited about what you're building," she says.

Just as Draper is eager to partner with founders from all corners of the market, she also thinks founders need to be open to every potential opportunity. "When you go out and fund, you should just plan on pitching at least 100 people. And I think a lot of people will come to me and say 'Everyone said no.' And I want to know, 'how many people did you talk to?' They might say, 'Eight.' You need to talk to 100. I pitched 500 people for my first fund and closed maybe 50 of them."

Even when potential investors say no, they still may come in later or be helpful in other ways. Shift your mindset to look at pitching as an opportunity to meet people.

"I give out my email addresses to like thousand-person rooms that I speak to. I just know that you have to create a pipeline," Draper explained. A lot of this comes back to the network-building we talked about in chapter 2. Once you start pitching, those investors become part of your extended network. An investor who is impressed by your pitch but already committed to funding a similar company might introduce you to someone with more bandwidth; an investor who passes now might start following your brand's press, waiting to see how sales look before coming back to the table. By putting yourself out there and constantly network-ing, you're increasing the possibility of doors opening down the road—even ones you wrote off or weren't expecting.

Again, this is where doing your due diligence in every aspect of your business pays off. By the time you're pitching outside funders, especially at the VC level, your pitches, marketing and brand identity should be solid, polished and impressive. Think of this process like you would applying for college, or even dating—plenty of people will say no, but ultimately you only need one yes. And when that yes is on the horizon, you need to be ready to grab it.

Securing VC money can be a huge advantage for your company, but it's also not the only way to make it work. In fact, some founders want to avoid VC money and money from investors who aren't already part of their inner circle, instead using a method known as "bootstrapping."

The appeal of bootstrapping is obvious—it might mean way more work and growing slowly, but it also means that your company is *yours*.

Eleven years ago, Rosie Johnston started mixing her own perfumes when the kinds of clean, fresh scents she wanted to wear seemed impossible to find on store shelves. Also interested in nontoxic, sustainable ingredients, Johnston's friends quickly convinced her that this was a product she could sell.

At first, Johnston wasn't sure what she wanted the financials of her fragrance line, By Rosie Jane, to look like. We've known each other for years, and when she was a guest on my podcast in March of 2021 she shared a funny story about inadvertently becoming a bootstrapper:

"I asked [my husband's friend], 'Will you lend me 2,500 bucks so that I can buy some packaging and stuff to sell this fragrance? I'll give you a 20 percent stake in the company.' And he said no! So I was like, 'All right, well, I'll just do it anyway.' And so we didn't do the box. And then I thought, 'It's probably more eco-friendly not to do a box.' So we did a swing tag. I had little stickers printed at Kinko's, and that was the beginning."

Now that By Rosie Jane is stocked at Sephora and regularly name-checked in the biggest fashion and beauty magazines, I can only imagine her husband's friend wishes he had taken that deal. But for Johnston, it planted the seeds of what doing it on her own could look like and, years later, she knows she made the right choice to keep the business mostly self-funded.

"We're kind of on this journey," she told me, "and it just didn't feel like who I am as a person to suddenly take what feels like a very organic and really kind of cool story about the way that we create products and the timeline that we do it, to suddenly just jump in and be like, 'Okay, you know what? Now we have 50 different sets, and we have 100 different fragrances.'"

Now, if you want to make 100 different fragrances, you may have no choice but to take on outside funding. And it might not feel like a burden at all, especially if going big has always been part of your plan. But for someone like Johnston, the money may well have meant more pressure to deviate from what makes her brand unique and could very easily have led her to burn out.

Here's another example of a brand I love that is blazing its own trail when it comes to funding.

It's hard to think of an industry growing as fast as the pet care space. People love their pets and are increasingly interested in what they're consuming—if you only eat organic food, why shouldn't your cat? If harsh shampoos irritate your sensitive skin, doesn't your dog deserve something just as gentle? Coupled with the spike in pet adoptions that occurred during the COVID-19 pandemic, it's a segment of the retail market that's only going to become more competitive.

Kim Hehir is the cofounder of Brutus Broth, a sustainable brand that produces bone broth and bone broth–based biscuits for dogs. Started in 2017, Brutus Broth's products are made in USDA-approved facilities, and their formulas are targeted to improve overall dog health and immune system response. Essentially, it's taking all the things humans love about bone broth, which we've been drinking for centuries, and sharing some of those benefits with four-legged friends.

When it comes to funding, Hehir explained on my podcast, "We've been kind of bootstrapping it. We've had some opportunities with companies to come in, but to be honest, unless it's a strategic investor, it's not interesting to us. And you know, we did a small friends and family round. We'll be doing another friends and family round, because it's expensive to pay for the inventory to supply Target!"

In Hehir's case, expensive is good, because it means big-name retailers have come calling. Specifically, a certain bull's-eye big-box store where well-heeled women shop for their dogs and for limited-edition collections from their favorite fashion designers said Hehir. "We launched in Target in March and it's what keeps me up at night because even though people are like, 'Oh my God, you're in Target. That's amazing!' We always say, 'It's one thing to get on the shelf. But the real work starts once you're on the shelf.'"

However you fund, that's a great piece of advice—one you should be coming back to even when you're in your dream stores or on the Instagram accounts of your favorite actresses. So many people make the mistake of thinking funding itself is the be-all and end-all—but that couldn't be further from the truth.

Having a great idea is one thing. Having a great business plan is another. Both of those things are key to getting any kind of funding, but what happens once the deposits actually hit your account? Taking the time to understand how finance works *now* will pay major dividends down the road.

8

A GOOD IDEA IS NEVER ENOUGH
(OR: WHY MARKETING MAKES ALL
THE DIFFERENCE)

Over the course of my time as an angel investor, I've seen some truly remarkable products—things that I know could be successful. But having a brilliant product isn't everything. There have been times when I looked at a company's marketing plan, talked to the founder about their vision for marketing the product and long-term success and said to myself, *It's too bad, but this is never going to work.*

Too many founders fall prey to the fantasy of "if you build it, they will come." The idea that your product alone speaks for itself, and all you have to do is make it. This is especially true in the age of social media, where anyone with more than a few hundred Instagram followers thinks they're a branding expert. I know from experience that that's not true—when I first started my podcast, it was sometimes hard to even get my friends to leave reviews. That isn't because I don't have great friends who support me—they do! But no one cares about your business as much as you do, and thinking that because someone supports you as a person, they'll automatically be a great supporter of your brand? That's a mistake.

Marketing is just as important as the product itself. Sometimes it's even more important—think about something like bottled water. Grocery stores stock hundreds of different brands, but you're probably loyal to one. Why? You might tell me it tastes better, or the bottle is easier to handle or the source of the water itself is more sustainable. But how do you know all of that? Because of *marketing*.

Marketing is the story you tell about your brand and your product, and getting that story right can be the difference between hitting the big time or never getting off the ground.

As you start to develop a marketing strategy, there are a few clarifying questions I find helpful to ask:

- What is your core mission?
- What are your brand's values?
- What's truly important to you?
- What unique value do you bring to your clients?

If you can't answer those questions right now, it's not the end of the world—it just means you have to spend more time digging into who you are as a brand and what you can offer your customers.

What is your brand's mission and what does it value?

Coral Chung, founder and CEO of Senreve, whose upscale, professional clothes are worn by women in cities around the world, finds that it's helpful to center her brand's values whenever she's launching a new product or working on a new advertising campaign. "We feel like it's really important as a brand to contribute and to really support women because one of the main brand pillars for us is empowerment," she told me on the podcast. "And I think it's always really important to be authentic and live up to those brand values."

From there, she's able to expand her brand's mission and its ideals: "One of our big cultural values at Senreve is optimism, flexibility, grit and perseverance. Those are some of our cultural values. And I think it really is important to focus on the silver lining and the positive through challenge. If you are able to pull through and survive, sometimes the best ideas and the most interesting things come out of that."

By starting with simple definitions of what's important to her brand and what's important to her customers, Chung has laid the framework for her brand's identity, making it easy for anyone working on marketing products, like advertisements or design presentations, to make Senreve's signature point of view clear at every step of the way.

Brooke Harris of Goodmylk has a similar ethos. "Our bigger goal is certainly to sell plant-based milk," she shared, "but because of my journey, we want to empower people on their own wellness journey, and really empower people to understand the food that they're putting into their mouth. And hopefully that will help make bigger changes in the food system, which is so messed up."

There's the elevator pitch, not for her product but for her brand itself. Yes, she's selling plant-based milk, but she's also selling empowerment: the idea that you can, and should, take your health and wellness goals into your own hands by learning about what's in the food you consume so that you can make more informed choices.

Suze Schwartz has her own story:

"I have a mission, and the mission is to share meditation far and wide with as many people as possible and show them just how easy it is to incorporate it into their everyday life. That's my goal. I want to do this on a huge scale. I think if everybody meditated, the world would be a much better place. So that's my goal. And I'm not going to stop until I achieve my goal."

If those three anecdotes—from Chung, Harris and Schwartz—sound similar, that's a good thing! Each of these women sits at the head of a fast-growing company that people want to buy from and be in business with, and they started by asking some of the same questions I posed to you above. Who are they? What are their values? What are their goals? When you can clearly define those things, you can begin to tell the story of your product in a way people will authentically connect with.

"The advice I would give for people starting a new brand," Vera Koch of eSalon and Colorsmith told me when we talked about the importance of a brand's story, "would be that it all starts with the story that you're looking to tell because that is what makes your brand differentiated, distinct and interesting. So build your core brand values, build the mission of what you're looking to accomplish and the needs that you're looking to fulfill. And then you can start to get the word out there. And my recommendation would be to always test different angles."

That means that your core story, your core identity, is the same, but it adapts and shifts depending on who you're talking to and what problem you're trying to solve.

Telling Your Story

Let's go back to the story of Kim Hehir and Brutus Bone Broth. Kim is far from the first person to think about dog food in an upscale way, so how was she going to establish her product as essential to would-be buyers?

"Our positioning is that we feel you shouldn't have to be a millionaire to feed your dog good food," she told me. "One of the things that we wanted to do is to bring affordable, accessible nutrition to the everyday consumer. We do get the raw feeders...bone broth is a building block of a raw food diet. So you're getting people who are raw feeders, who would never shop in a pet aisle, going into the pet aisle now, looking for our product. Or you get people who have been feeding their dog kibble, who could never afford a raw food diet [and] are like, 'Oh, I can afford this. And this is giving my dog that little extra something.' It's like giving your kid a multivitamin."

And just like that, Hehir has come up with one story that speaks to two customers. Now, these customers both have something in common, which is that they care about their dogs, and they want to be feeding them the best food. But from there, they split: Customer A is a person who already feeds their dog raw food. Maybe they even make it by hand! To them, Hehir's product is a time saver. It's a way to continue caring for their dog like they care for themselves while outsourcing some of the work to a brand they trust. Customer B may not have even heard of raw food diets for dogs (or humans, for that matter) before happening upon Brutus Bone Broth. But just like Customer A, they love their four-legged friend and are excited to move beyond the world of standard wet and dry food to show their pets a little extra love.

Hehir's marketing plan has homed in on a broad trend—dog lovers—and found ways to make her product appeal to subsets of that first group. Without a robust marketing plan—let's say she just thought "anyone who loves dogs will love this product"—she'd actually be losing out on business from both segments. Customer A would never even know about her because they don't shop in the readymade pet-food aisle. And Customer B might see her broth on the shelves and just keep walking: without the brand education, they'd have no way of knowing how her product was different from the other dog food on store shelves.

Finding Your Customers

Thinking about specific individuals and how you might solve their problems is hugely important, especially in industries like fashion. The average department store carries hundreds (sometimes even thousands) of brands. And for the average shopper who may not have the time—or the emotional fortitude—to spend an entire Saturday trying on jeans, you need to make it clear that *your* jeans fit into *her* life.

Veronica Beard is a super chic, super fun fashion line designed by Veronica Miele Beard and Veronica Swanson Beard (they're sisters-in-law who married a set of brothers). The Veronicas attribute much of their success to the fact that they aren't necessarily designing for *all* women but for the Veronica Beard woman. "I think that we really know our customer," said Veronica M. Beard on my podcast, "and our mission has stayed the same. We design clothes that are hardwired for real life. That's what we always say. So we design what we want to wear, and we're so in tune with our customer. We know what she's doing...What's going on in her life."

Veronica S. Beard added: "And (we know) what's missing from the market...We're problem junkies...We're always on the hunt. And it's like, I really want my jeans to fit like this. I can't find them and the fabrics suck. We're the girl that we're designing for."

Rather than try to think about jeans that would please everyone (a fool's errand if there ever was one), the Veronicas instead envisioned their ideal client and then made the jeans she would want. They knew from their research, both professional and personal, that their type was a common one in the stores they wanted to be in, so they established first that there was a market and a place for them in it.

Then they designed the product that solved their ideal consumer's problems.

Okay, you might be thinking: I know my product is great, and I know exactly who my target customer is, but how do I find her?

That's a great question, especially if you're just starting out. Big brands can partner with celebrities and take out full-page advertisements in *Marie Claire* and *Martha Stewart Living*, but for most new businesses, especially ones in the bootstrapping or prefunding stages, you're going to have to get a little more creative.

The first step is being honest about who you want to sell to. If the answer is "everyone," you're thinking too broadly.

When I sat down with Tamra Johnson of Flex-Team, she talked about this issue: "Getting the clients I think is often a challenge in a business, but I would say even more specifically, really refining what it is you're selling, and being super focused on what it is you're selling," she said. "If you're too general in what you're offering, you are not at the top of anyone's mind ever, for anything. Don't be afraid to get really, really specific on the services that you're offering, and know that that's actually going to make the job of selling easier than harder."

Just because something sounds niche doesn't mean it won't have real reach—after all, would you rather buy from an expert, or from a generalist who is throwing things at the wall hoping something sticks?

Taking Control of the Narrative

If you're at the forefront of a new trend, finding customers might actually look like establishing your brand as an educator and yourself (the CEO) as a thought leader.

As the founder of W!nk, the nation's first therapeutic cannabis line created by women, for women, Stacy Verbeist knew a huge part of her marketing was going to be explaining to people that their preconceived notions about cannabis and cannabis-based products were due for an overhaul.

"We did what's called a deskside," she explained.

"And that's where you travel to the different magazines, and you bring your whole collection with you, and you present it to them. And then we'd always give them a sample gift pack of different items that they could try out, and they could write about. Our big goal was going out there and educating writers and PR people on how to relay the message to the customer on why CBD can be so effective."

Think about how big CBD is now and also about what a fringe idea it was even a few years ago. It's so ubiquitous now mainly due to entrepreneurs like Verbeist, who had the foresight to see that good marketing was going to mean thorough education.

When it came to pitching directly to customers, Verbeist was also up against some very real government regulations.

"Because the FDA does not approve cannabis for advertising," she told me, "it's really hard for companies [like ours] to really grow their sales at a rapid pace. For us, everything has been on education. We really pride ourselves in every post that we do by educating the customer on what they're getting, and what might help with any kind of ailments they have."

By talking to her customers first as people who want to know more about cannabis and who could benefit from her products in ways they might not know yet, she's establishing trust and establishing W!nk as a go-to resource for questions on a product that might be new to a lot of potential buyers.

That means keeping the lines of communication between her company and her customers open.

"We are big on social media, and just posting products and how they relate to the customers. We do a lot of digital marketing," she said. "We work with a lot of influencers and we just started upping our SEO (Search Engine Optimization) to build our eCommerce business. Because of COVID, a lot of our retailers have shut down. So right now we're just going direct to consumers. I think it's just all education. We've got a 36 percent repeat customer rate online, which is fabulous."

Verbeist's business is far from the only one impacted by the COVID-19 pandemic. But in her case, W!nk had already put in the time to build a network online, working with influencers to get the product onto the screens of customers and being willing to have open conversations about what her cannabis-based products can do. That meant that when lots of brands were scrambling to adapt to marketing mostly (or solely) online, she was already ahead of the game.

It's also worth thinking about whether or not your marketing plan should include the idea of buzz—and if so, how are you going to create it? On one memorable episode of the podcast, I sat down with Sheila Morovati, founder of nonprofit organizations Crayon Collection and Habits of Waste, which focus on repurposing and reducing waste for environmental protection. Nonprofit marketing can be tough because the field is crowded, so grabbing the spotlight is especially important.

"Part of my philosophy about environmentalism and running a nonprofit is that we need people to participate," Morovati told me. "My organizations, both of them, are global organizations—if you're a human being on this planet, you can participate essentially. And that's our goal, is to get loud and to let everybody know."

So how was Morovati going to make a splash?

"We decided to set a Guinness World Record! Because, yet again, it's back-to-school time, and yet again, so many children are going to school without the supplies they need," she said. "So we decided to donate the most crayons in history. And we did 1,009,500 crayons to 700 teachers in LAUSD schools."

Morovati's world record served a few purposes: first, it got crayons into the hands of kids, which is her ultimate mission, but it also made the news and established her nonprofit as the one to contact for companies that want to get involved with school supplies. Now she counts national restaurant chains like Denny's among her partners and uses her website to make it easy for anyone who has access to crayons to make donations.

Social Media: Making It Work for You

For Coral Chung, social media is a way for Senreve to not just showcase new designs but to build a community of the brand's loyal fans. "We focus a lot on developing content and curating that and making sure that it's aligned with our brand," she said. "It's about creating a community where there are very loyal and fanatically enthusiastic people about the brand and about the product's course. And social media kind of accelerates that, and gives a great platform to continue developing that."

By posting regular content designed to speak directly to her customers, she's able to position Senreve almost as a friend, an identity whose pictures you might favorite on Instagram just as you'd favorite the pictures of someone you knew in real life. One thing Chung smartly takes advantage of is the fact that social media allows brands to showcase a whole swath of customers:

"We want as much representation and diversity as possible [in our social media marketing posts]," she said. Senreve's social media presence looks like their client base, which in turn gives their marketing a seamless feel that keeps customers engaged.

Speaking of engagement, one big mistake brands make on social media is simply posting content and letting it sit there for users to interact with.

Why is this bad? Well, in letting content sit there, you lose the opportunity to start a conversation and create a position of authority for your brand. A skincare company that actively creates content and captions that lead to conversations on environmentally friendly packaging quickly becomes the authority on sustainable skincare. That means consumers are more likely to remember and seek them out, versus a clean beauty skincare brand that simply posts content but does not talk about their initiatives. Set yourself up for success by writing and sharing content that sparks discussion and gives you the opportunity to stand out by sharing valuable insight with your consumers. Set up an affiliate program so people learn about your brand not just from you but also from influencers who cultivate followings and can share your products—and how great they are—with audiences who rely on them for guidance. This builds trust, and trust builds loyalty, which are the two goals of any good marketing plan.

9

CONSIDER DIRECT SALES

Do you want to become a CEO, or be your own boss on your own time but don't have the capital—or you can't quit your day job just yet? I've found the perfect opportunity for you. It's low investment and low risk, but you are in business for yourself, immediately making money. Remember Gregg Renfrew? She's the reason I'm about to tell you something that might surprise you: as you're thinking about building a brand and a business, consider working with a direct sales company (also known as "multilevel marketing," or MLM).

MLMs get a bad rap—think about every "hey, girl!" message you've ever gotten from an old high school classmate, or the exposés about predatory companies and people who wanted to "get rich quick" now stuck with garages full of inventory they can't move. Trust me, I get it—when I told people I was investing and joining as a consultant in a direct sales company, a lot of them thought I was crazy.

Direct selling is not like that anymore. Gone are the days of stocking inventory in your garage and hosting home parties for friends and neighbors. We live in the side hustle times, where tons of people have a side gig to supplement their regular income. If there's one thing you should have learned during the pandemic, it's this: don't rely on one stream of income! You never know when that will stop. So direct sales or MLM is a great way to supplement your income or even replace your income on your terms. There are so many legitimately great companies—with legitimately great products—getting into the direct sales game. Last year alone, direct sellers in the United States represented nearly $40 billion in business and nearly six million direct sellers (close to a million doing it full-time) sold products to almost 30 million customers. It's also worth pointing out that 74 percent of direct sellers are women.

One of my investments was in the friend and family round of Beautycounter. When the company launched, I decided to try my hand in direct selling, too. Although I had not tried direct selling before, I believed in the product. Once I joined as an independent consultant, I quickly realized I was the CEO of my own company. How I organized my business and team was like running a company. The beauty of direct selling was that there was limited risk, and I received a paycheck the first month. Having started many companies before and studied entrepreneurship in business school, I knew that it takes three to five years to become profitable in a start-up with about a 10 percent chance of success. In no other industry can a CEO invest under $1000 to launch a business, work on their own terms and have the ability to make seven figures. Trust me: it's hard work, and it's not for everyone, but if you are willing to run your direct selling business like a real company, you potentially can become part of the two percent club. To this day, I don't understand why more people don't choose this route over starting their own corporation.

Here's Beautycounter's CEO, Gregg Renfrew, on the business:

"All of us are talking about the fact that the future of commerce specific to beauty is going to continue to be direct-to-consumer. I think the wholesalers in general are in a lot of trouble right now. I hope some of them weather the storm. I think some of them will not, unfortunately. Being able to have a direct dialogue with your client, and for us our two clients, our clients who are [also] independent consultants, is critical today and will be in the future months and years," Renfrew recently shared in an interview about the future of the beauty industry. It makes perfect sense: if you're a manufacturer, wouldn't you rather have a product being sold by people who can speak to the benefits and the results in a meaningful way, and if you're a buyer, wouldn't you rather buy from a person rather than an advertisement or an algorithm?

It's obviously paying off: Beautycounter now has more than 44,000 consultants in the United States and Canada. And their current annual revenue of $325 million is sure to grow as people recognize the unique opportunities of direct selling.

Okay, you might be thinking, I still really want to pursue my own business idea, so why not do direct selling to learn some business skills while you develop your own idea? Below I discuss five big takeaways from being a CEO of your own direct selling business. You may also find that you love direct selling so much that there is no need to pursue launching your own company. But if not, and you still want to follow your dream, the insight and knowledge you gain from your direct selling business while you develop your own idea will be invaluable.

First, direct selling has a long history of offering sales and business experience to people who might not otherwise be able to access that knowledge.

Direct sales as we know it today got its start with a divorced single mom named Brownie Wise. A former saleswoman for Stanley Home Products, she started hosting informal parties. The guests were mostly fellow moms and, crucially, people Wise knew socially or from her neighborhood. She organized games, provided snacks and sold Tupperware, a then-revolutionary storage product that made it easy to save and reuse leftovers. Wise quickly proved that selling Tupperware via home parties to people in her network —which was constantly growing thanks to word of mouth—was more profitable than selling the products in stores, which quickly caught the attention of Earl Tupper, the inventor of Tupperware. Wise was hired to create an exclusive home parties division of the company, where she invented much of the direct sales playbook still in use today: find people who want to sell and have a mind for business, teach them about the product and offer them incentives to make sales. Wise, in 1954, was the first woman to appear on the cover of *Business Week* and is credited with pioneering a new kind of corporate culture—one in which things like being a mom, being a homemaker and being friendly translated to actual business success.

Beauty, like Tupperware, has long been an industry in which direct sales naturally thrives. From Avon to Mary Kay, women around the world, many of whom might not otherwise have worked at all (let alone made the kind of money some direct sales consultants make), were able to channel their natural ambition into business, in large part because many of them were *already experts on the marketplace.*

The average woman in America will spend close to $20,000 on makeup in her lifetime. And since that's just the average, we can infer that millions of women spend close to that each year on makeup, hair care and skincare. If you're one of those women, there's a good chance you're pretty savvy about the industry—what really works, what ingredients are just marketing, what products irritate sensitive skin and how a routine might need to change as someone ages. The community-based environment of direct sales companies like Beautycounter means consultants can draw upon that learned knowledge while they're selling. It also means the channels of communication between consultants and the people who work in research, development and corporate branding are more open than they often are at companies with a more regimented business model. "The most impactful highlights have come from our customers' appreciation and feedback. I receive personal notes from both our independent consultants and clients about how our products are not only changing their skin, but more importantly their lives by providing more protection for themselves and their families. As a direct retail brand, we offer unique and powerful financial opportunities for women who join our mission as Beautycounter consultants. I have really enjoyed seeing how our business model and this opportunity has empowered women," Gregg Renfrew told The Huffington Post in 2014. As a company focused on clean beauty, Beautycounter has involved consultants in almost every aspect of advocating for healthier products and more stringent guidelines for the industry —when Renfrew spoke on Capitol Hill, she was accompanied by working Beautycounter consultants. That level of access, and the ability to see firsthand what it looks like at the top of a company, is something much harder to come by as an entry-level employee at a traditional corporate job.

You may not be interested in beauty. That's okay. I wasn't either. Since I am passionate about health and wellness, I loved the idea that Beautycounter was providing cleaner products in the personal care industry. *I* love eating clean and staying healthy, which is why Beautycounter initially appealed to me: after all, if I don't want preservatives and chemicals in my food, why would I want them in my mascara? I was so impressed with the mission that I became an investor in the company.

Find *your* passion and find a direct sales company that sells products that aligns with it. If you are into essential oils, there is a company for that. If you are into fitness there is a company for that—or cooking, supplements or modest fashion? The list goes on and on. If you are passionate about the product, you aren't just selling, you are sharing your passion. Before Beautycounter, I never did cold calling or learned the ins and outs of sales. Joining a direct retail company will allow you to learn sales and marketing. Who knows, you might be so good at it that you decide to forgo your business idea and do your direct sales business full time.

The second thing I love about direct sales as a business opportunity is that it comes with readymade products and a marketing strategy.

When starting a company everything takes twice as long and twice as much time as you think. There are so many things that can go wrong. The labels are printed wrong, the wrong bottles are shipped, laws change that affect your business: the list is endless. The great thing about joining a direct selling company is that you don't have to worry about these problems. As the CEO of your company you only need to worry about recruiting a great team and then selling the products. By experiencing the many problems that arise as an independent consultant, you will learn from mistakes on someone else's dollar when you start your company. Or maybe you will realize you don't want to deal with problems every day and so decide to stick to being CEO of your direct selling brand.

Your parent company will also be responsible for launching new products and providing marketing and training for your team. Let's take a look at Beautycounter again. They are always coming up with the latest and greatest cosmetics and personal care products. They spend the necessary time and money researching and testing each new product. You don't need to have to worry about any of this. You just need to share with your clients when it launches.

Think of it this way: if Beautycounter, a company with products beloved by makeup artists and regular people alike, is launching a new eyeshadow palette, everyone who loves Beautycounter will want to buy that eyeshadow palette. And if you're the person they buy this product from, that means guaranteed traffic to your business, at which point you'll also get the chance to sell them other products. That's what direct sales offers: they provide the products and the brand name, and you provide the drive, the team and the sales.

One of the hardest aspects of launching a business is the sheer amount of time, money and know-how it can take to handle the actual branding and marketing. Remember when I was working at my sewing machine, monogramming the kinds of kids' clothes that now regularly appear on lifestyle blogs and in magazines? I had the product, but I didn't have the infrastructure. Direct sales provides both: let's say you try a Beautycounter serum, and almost instantly you know it's one of your new Holy Grail skincare items. You know that you love it, but how are you going to tell other people about it? How are you going to spread the word beyond your friends or your workplace network? A company like Beautycounter has millions of dollars and an entire team available to produce advertising that works and to develop strategic partnerships with influencers and stores like Target. That means that before you've even sold your first item, there's a group of people who want to buy it. It also means that if a company is launching a new product, people will be waiting to buy it before it even goes on sale. Even though you may not directly get the sales, the increased brand recognition will make it easier for you to sell to your customers. One of Gregg Renfrew's frequent quotes is "a rising tide raises all ships." She talks about the time Geico launched a national ad that initially upset the individually owned branches of Geico, but these independent owners quickly realized their sales were increasing—in addition to the direct corporate sales—because of the increased brand recognition.

I don't mean to suggest that direct sales is "easy money"—we all know there's really no such thing. Successful consultants are people who put in the work of learning about the product, developing their networks and dedicating time and energy to their businesses. They hustle and are not afraid to hear the word "no."

"When you start a new business, you need to prepare yourself that it will require an incredible amount of work and commitment, and it will not happen overnight. It will take patience, dedication and perseverance to make it a success. And be prepared to give up sleep," Gregg Renfrew told The Huffington Post. "However, I don't think there is a perfect recipe. I try to wake up an hour before the rest of my house to have a little time for myself, whether that is to read, go for a hike, or snuggle with whichever child snuck into bed during the night. I will also spend that time getting my children's lunches ready and making sure their breakfast is made so I can enjoy it with them before the craziness of the day begins."

That brings us to another reason I recommend looking into direct sales if what you're after is the chance to develop the leadership and management part of your brain: *building a downline, setting a schedule and doing the work of selling all mirror things you'd do at various career moments in a regular office.*

In most direct sales organizations, you sell products, but you also build what the industry calls a downline, which is a lot like the team you'd build if you were starting your own company. At first, you start slow— picking one or two people to sign up under you, training them, mentoring them and working with them as a team. When they're ready, they'll start building downlines of their own, with you serving as a kind of grand boss to their team members.

It can be tempting to try to turn anyone who shows interest in your products into members of your downline, and that's what some direct sellers do. I'd argue, though, that the real value lies in doing it carefully: teaching yourself what it means to hire and what it means to manage with a group of people you'd want to hire and manage if you were running your own company and selling a product of your own invention. Some questions to ask yourself include:

- Is this person someone I can trust?
- Is this person motivated for the right reasons, or are they looking to get rich quick or coast on the hard work of other team members?
- Can this person offer a perspective I might not have in my orbit already? For example, if I'm great at talking to people in person but my social media presence could use some help, would it be smart to invest in someone who excels at using Instagram and other platforms?
- Do I envision wanting to spend a lot of

time with this person? Are they friendly or prickly, a talker or more reserved?

If you've read the rest of this book, you'll see that these are almost the exact same questions I'd ask about a person coming to work for me. While at a regular job, it might take you years to get to the point where you're making hiring decisions, in direct sales you start much earlier in your career—a huge advantage when it comes to building your identity as a businesswoman.

Talking about hiring brings us to the next area in which I think direct sales shines: *it's a business largely based on networks, which will teach you how to cultivate and harness the power of your own.*

"When I was thinking about launching Beautycounter, my first phone call was to my dear friend Patrick Davis, the founder and head partner of Davis Brand Capital. Over the past 15 years, he has provided sound advice within the areas of branding and marketing, but has also been an invaluable sounding board and resource to help me work through some of the biggest challenges in my career," explained Gregg Renfrew in a 2014 interview. It was a smart move— haven't we talked about how important it is to reach out to potential mentors from every part of your network?

But this also extends to Beautycounter consultants,

who are encouraged to lean on people both above and below them to train, problem solve, strategize and coordinate events to drive sales and grow their teams.

Direct sales is sometimes referred to as "network marketing" because it allows you to work within the network you already have—whatever that might look like. If you don't have networking experience, it can feel like "reach out to people you know, or that your friends know," is lofty advice geared toward people who went to elite schools and work in clubby industries like tech and finance. But with direct sales, people who are *already in your phone contacts list* can become customers, and people in their phone contacts list can become colleagues. Former coworkers, neighbors, extended family and yes, even people you lost touch with 15 years ago—especially now that so much of direct selling happens online and on social media—you don't need a fancy alumni network or a country club membership to make connections with people. Plus, since what you're selling is something you've already used, liked and educated yourself about, personal outreach feels even more natural. Where you might feel shy or awkward asking a friend to patronize your store or use your graphic design services, encouraging them to check out a new makeup line with tons of products under $50 feels less stressful—which means you'll do it more, learning about your business style and strategies each time.

Another reason I think direct sales can hugely benefit women who want to get started in business, or who want to get back into the world of business after taking time off, is that it's like micro-investing: *the start-up costs are significantly lower than the ones you'd incur starting a business from scratch, so you have space to innovate—and fail!—without staking your whole livelihood on it.*

Think about any of the successful businesswomen we've talked about in this book so far. All of them took significant risks. For them, it paid off. But not everyone wants to (or is able to) take those kinds of risks. Quite frankly, not everyone who has the drive and the skillset to be a CEO is *also* the kind of person who invents new hit products.

That's why I encourage women to consider looking at direct sales as a kind of micro investment: for a fraction of the cost (in both money, time and labor) of building your own company from scratch, you can start building a business in which someone else is doing things like researching formulas, designing packaging and setting a product rollout schedule. By the time an independent consultant is ready to sell, so much of the work that keeps businesses from getting off the ground in the first place has already been done.

That means direct sales consultants have the freedom to get creative with things like events, marketing, sales and platforms: think working with local community organizations to host fundraisers that also build awareness for your brand, partnering with independent boutiques to offer customers a space to try products before buying, or setting up accounts on new social platforms that aren't as tried and true as the big ones like Facebook. It also means that while you're learning about the building blocks of business, or flexing the business muscles you've been developing on your own or at a different job, you're able to use your own unique skills. A ton of makeup artists, for example, use their expertise to sell products, while someone with experience teaching might use what they've developed in the classroom to put together effective training manuals for their team. If you try something new, and it doesn't work out—something that happens to anyone with CEO ambitions—you've got the ability to go back to the drawing board with minimal stress.

Finally, I consider the most important reason direct retail is so compelling is the control of your own calendar. There's is a reason many direct sellers are women and moms—it's a business you can run from your phone, on your own time. A traditional company—even one you're the CEO of—often means adhering to traditional business hours and practices. However, in direct selling, you genuinely make your own hours and your own schedule. As I grew my Beautycounter business, I did it while my children napped or attended school. I would then respond to emails and do reach outs at night after my kids went to bed. I was able to grow my business on my time fitting it into the nooks and crannies of the day while waiting at school pickup or on my daily walk I could make a few calls or listen to training videos. Having the flexibility in your schedule to be anywhere at any time and still grow your business is something that you can't take lightly as an entrepreneur.

I never would have considered working with a direct retail company, but Gregg Renfrew's vision convinced me. Beautycounter as a product meets every expectation I have for a company: the product is great, the market is strong and the CEO is someone who knows what she's doing.

I've met so many wonderful women through my work with Beautycounter, and I'm proud to be on a team with them. And the people who thought I was crazy? They understand now what I saw in Beautycounter from the beginning and the opportunity that being an independent consultant provides.

CONCLUSION

When I started The Badass CEO podcast over a year ago, I did it to share my knowledge of angel investing while learning about other people's vision and passion for growing companies. I love to dive deep into the nitty gritty of a business and dissect what makes a business and a CEO beat the odds of failure to turn a company into a success. I thought The Badass CEO podcast was a perfect platform to share the information I learn each time I talk to a CEO as an angel investor and questions I ask when deciding whether I invest in a company. However, when I launched my podcast, I never knew about the low statistics that plague women CEOs and entrepreneurs. When I first heard that only 1.7 percent of women entrepreneurs ever reach $1 million in sales, I couldn't believe it. Then when I read the statistic that only five percent of CEOs are women,

I was even more shocked. After learning these stats, I decided it would be my mission to help other women reach their dreams of becoming a CEO either within a company or on their own and help their companies earn over $1 million in sales.

Sadly, there are too many reasons *why* these sales statistics are so, but I hope that've been able to shed some light on how to overcome common obstacles to success and change. We, as women, can't be everything to everyone all the time. We need to figure out what is important to us. The answer is personal, so no one can tell you what is important to you. It may be your career, your family, your health or your mission in life. Only you can decide. Once you choose, I challenge you to keep your foot on the gas and follow your dreams unapologetically. You will have doubters and naysayers along the way. You may even make enemies. Remember, you are charting a new path. It may be a new path for your family, an industry, a community or even an entire globe. No one may see what you see as the truth. Follow your truth because that is what makes leaders, innovators and Unicorn companies. A Unicorn company is a company that has a $1 billion valuation. Only 600 Unicorn companies exist worldwide. Beautycounter just became one this year.

So don't be afraid to follow your dreams and passions. That uneasiness you might feel is not imposter syndrome or lack of confidence. It is you challenging yourself to limits you are not comfortable with. To grow and excel, you need to get to that uneasy place more often than not. Get comfortable with that feeling. Take it on and own it. Don't forget to grab at least a mentor or two for the ride. It will make it easier to navigate and much more enjoyable.

As supermodel Molly Sims said on my podcast, "You have to have a strong passion, strong work ethic and you got to go for it."

Reach out to let me know when you reach that $1 million sales hurdle or become a CEO. I would love to share your story.

I wanted to elaborate on two real-life scenarios—one from a woman who is on her path to becoming a CEO and another from two business partners with different work styles and opinions who had to learn how to work together.

How to Conceptualize Fantasy Work Life

Example: this is from Tanya, 36, an aspiring executive development coach.

- What do I want my work days to look like?

I want to work four to five hours a day, early in the morning, and then be free by the afternoons. I want to work with up to two clients a day but not more than that, so I don't burn out.

- What sort of relationship do I want to have with my company?

I want my company to spark joy. I want to feel like every client I take on makes me a better choice, so I'm always growing and getting better.

- What are the responsibilities I want to take on?

I want to develop my own curriculum, which means I do my own research and writing. I want to build a sturdy but professional relationship with all my clients. I actually love social media, so I would want to develop my company's online voice and brand.

- What are the responsibilities I absolutely do not want to take on?

Anything having to do with payroll. I don't want to deal with editing audio or video. I'm bad at it, and it stresses me out. Any discussion of refunds or client dissatisfaction will need someone else in the mix. I know I can take those things very personally, which isn't helpful to the client.

- What sort of experience do I want consumers to have with my company/product/service?

I want my clients to feel like they already possess the tools to improve their work lives but just didn't know how to use them. I want to be considered a great resource.

- Who are the types of people that will work for my company?

People who are passionate about self-development, growth and feel like they have something to contribute to the world.

- What qualities will my best employees have?

They will have courage, honesty and be detail-focused.

- What qualities will my employees absolutely not have?

They will not be apathetic, close minded or dishonest.

- What sort of relationship do I want to have with my employees?

I hope I can be an inspiration for my employees. I also want to be a resource for them. I want them to be willing collaborators if I want to try out a curriculum with them.

- What does my time off from my job look like?

No screens. No calls. But I do want to use my off time to read, write and develop my curriculum. I also want to be able to go on a three-day retreat in the mountains and not worry that my business will fall apart.

- How do I want to feel about the work at the end of a week?

Excited for the next week to start!

- How do I want my family to feel about my work?

I want them to feel proud of me and not threatened or disrespected if I spend my off time developing curriculum. It nourishes me, and I want them to support that.

How to Conceptualize Fantasy Work Life with a Partner

Example: Stan and Marla are business partners who are launching a cruelty-free, all-vegan makeup line aimed at Gen Z-ers who may be using their allowance or summer jobs to buy lip gloss. Marla is a makeup artist with a large social media following, and Stan is her best friend of 15 years who has launched two successful streetwear businesses of his own. Here are some questions they should ask each other or have an outsider facilitate.

- What does a harmonious, productive business relationship look like for each partner?
- What are Veronica's dream qualities she wants in a business partner? What are Stan's?
- Do these qualities exist in Stan and in Marla separately?
- What are the qualities each partner

absolutely does *not* want in a business partner?

- Do these qualities exist in Stan and in Marla?
- What is the best possible outcome for our business? Are both partners willing to sell when the business is in its prime?
- What will a sale of the company mean for our partnership?
- What will it mean for our relationship?
- What's the worst possible outcome for this business?
- How will that outcome impact our relationship?
- What are the expectations Stan has of Veronica in launching their business?
- What are the expectations Veronica has of Stan?
- What expectations can they both agree to?
- What are the expectations they have of their employees?
- Who makes the final decision when you don't agree?

How to Define Goals, Roles and Processes in a Team

Let's continue to use Stan and Marla to illustrate how this checklist can work. Here are their answers:

Goals:

- What is our shared purpose?

We believe vegan makeup should be affordable, fashionable, and the first choice for a new generation of savvy shoppers who know that quality can and should exist without cruelty.

- What is our ideal outcome?

We inspire a new generation of consumers to reach for vegan cosmetic products first. We want our company to become profitable within three years. We want our company to successfully scale so we can invest in other cruelty-free, like-minded ventures.

- What metrics do we use for success?

We will focus on two metrics: sales and social media engagement. We want to make sure we are reaching a younger audience, and the best way to do that is reaching them on the platforms they use.

Roles:

- What are each person's responsibilities on the team?

Stan is responsible for all things data, sales and business development related. Marla is responsible for brand, product testing, social media and design.

- In what areas do we have autonomy in decision-making?

While we will consult and collaborate as often as possible, there is a clear separation between business development and brand development. Anything that has to do with money, investors and data analysis is Stan. Marla has final say on anything outward facing to consumers.

- In what areas is there a single person who decides?

Ultimately the buck stops with Stan because he has a bigger stake in our company.

Process:

- How do we plan?

We meet three times a week, with an agenda, and we make all big decisions by phone or in person, and then we memorialize it in email. In the past we relied a lot more on email but found that asynchronous communication led to misunderstandings. Both of us hate taking notes, but we understand they are necessary. We record our in-person meetings, then hire a transcription service to type it up. It's a bit of a luxury expense, but it's cheaper than an administrative assistant!

- How often do we revisit and refine metrics we use for success?

Every quarter and never before. We both have the tendency to get reactive so we stick to this system so we can enforce patience.

- What do we do when we meet a milestone of benchmark?

We buy cheap champagne to celebrate, and then we make sure to put aside time to debrief about why we were successful. We go through decision points and reflect on what we did well and what could be improved upon. We are constantly trying to extract lessons so we can invest in getting better.

- What happens when we are behind schedule?

We do everything we can to not cut corners. We will forgo activities that don't have to do with work, and we work weekends. We never want to undermine our product. After we ship or deliver we make time to reflect on why we got behind and learn how to avoid doing it again.

Interpersonal

What are our shared expectations with each other?

- *We have five expectations that we wrote out and have laminated on our wall: 1) Lead with kindness. 2) Embrace failure. 3) Consult the pillow when angry, frustrated or sad—that means sleep on it! 4) No texting, emailing or scrolling during our in-person or Zoom meetings. If we're distracted then we're undermining our work. 5) We are the only two decision makers in this company: that means significant others, best friends, parents or random internet commenters don't get to weigh in on strategy.*

How do we resolve conflict?

- *We like to say that we embrace conflict! We both have big ideas and big personalities. Having strong opinions and strong reactions to things isn't a bad thing even if it gets heated, but it can never be personal. It should always be about ideas. If one of us gets bruised, then we have to say it out loud and the other person is expected not to push back, explain or minimize. Instead the offender should take responsibility for doing better.*

THE BADASS CEO BOOK BONUS MATERIALS

Scan this code for supplemental videos and resources to compliment *The Badass CEO* book.

ACKNOWLEDGMENTS

To my children Mac, Gretchen, Tucker, Kit and Lilly, who inspire me every day to be a better person and mother. I am so blessed to have you in my life.

To my husband Malcolm, who I met at my first day at work at Kidder Peabody and knew at that moment I would marry. You have been my biggest cheerleader ever since.

To my dad, who was a savvy businessman and the smartest person I have ever known. You taught me so much about business, to never rely on one stream of income and that family is the most important asset in life. I miss you every day.

To my brothers Rich, Brendian and Craig for the lifetime of memories and laughs and for keeping it real.

To Suzy, my big sister who taught me so much about life and to be grateful for who I am. I miss you so much and hope you are making Dad laugh like you always did.

To my mom, who juggled raising six kids and a real estate business.

To the rest of my fr-amily, who keep life fun and challenge me to "Never take the foot off the gas!"

To my Badass community and all the Badass CEOs I have interviewed. Thank you for believing in me and supporting me along the way.

To Anna David and her team...Thank you for making this dream possible.

To my team, Nina, PJ, Pilar and the Elevate Group who help me get it all done!

I love you all.

ABOUT THE AUTHOR

Mimi MacLean is an angel investor who focuses on female-led companies with something to say. A mom of five, she's also a CPA, a Columbia Business School graduate and the host of The Badass CEO, a weekly podcast where she interviews entrepreneurs and high-level executives to discuss business strategies, life experiences and what a Badass CEO needs to know. As the founder of the Happy Birthday Foundation, MacLean works to ensure children in need get to celebrate their birthdays with joy, love and presents.

She lives in Connecticut with her husband and five children.

Made in the USA
Middletown, DE
04 January 2023

20991202R00109